WebAssembly 2.0 Essentials

AF515648

Second Edition

Making Migrations, Cloud-Native Integration, and Production-Ready WebAssembly Applications Easier

Emrys Callahan

Copyright © 2025 by GitforGits

All rights reserved. This book is protected under copyright laws and no part of it may be reproduced or transmitted in any form or by any means, electronic or mechanical, including photocopying, recording, or by any information storage and retrieval system, without the prior written permission of the publisher. Any unauthorized reproduction, distribution, or transmission of this work may result in civil and criminal penalties and will be dealt with in the respective jurisdiction at anywhere in India, in accordance with the applicable copyright laws.

Published by: GitforGits

Publisher: Sonal Dhandre

www.gitforgits.com

Printed in India

First Printing: October 2025

ISBN: 978-93-49174-46-7

Cover Design by: Kitten Publishing

Disclaimer:

This book, including all its text, diagrams, and illustrations, is an original work developed for educational and informational purposes. The content is not affiliated with, endorsed by, or sponsored by any other company, brand, or entity referenced within. All brand names, product names, and trademarks mentioned are the property of their respective owners and are used in a descriptive, educational context only. Every effort has been made to ensure that no copyrighted or trademarked material has been copied or misused in this book. All diagrams and illustrations that are not original have been used with proper attribution and credit to their respective sources.

If we believe that any content in this book infringes upon the copyright or trademark, please contact us immediately at support@gitforgits.com. Upon notification, corrective action will be taken promptly.

Prologue

The first edition of WebAssembly Essentials was released, and I was unsure how people would react. But the response was amazing. It was so encouraging to see developers from startups to enterprise teams getting in touch. They shared how they'd built faster applications, moved critical systems and achieved performance they didn't think was possible. That feedback was really important. However, along with the success came repeated requests: "Can you show us how to move our current code to a new system?" "What about using Wasm in Kubernetes?" "How do we use modern cloud-based tools?" I listened, took notes, and realised that this second edition needed to be more than just an update because it had to deal with the real challenges you face today.

The latest version of WebAssembly has arrived and it has some really cool new features. I knew that I had to completely rewrite this book to make sure it was up to date. Now, here we are. Within this book, I will take you from the very basics of memory, control flow, and the mechanics that make Wasm work, through to compiling multiple languages, building multi-threaded applications, and optimising for real-world performance. But we won't stop there.

If you follow the steps, you'll see exactly how to move your Wasm 1.0 projects to version 2.0 without stopping your current production. I'll show you how to integrate with Dapr for distributed systems and deploy on Kubernetes with confidence. All the examples come from real work, real problems I've solved or helped others solve. There is no unnecessary information, and no complicated, theoretical ideas. It has just practical code and simple explanations that don't waste your time.

I wrote this book to help you avoid the mistakes I made when I was just starting out. It will show you how to go from being a beginner to being a WebAssembly developer who is ready to start producing things.

Let's get started and build something amazing together.

— Emrys Callahan

Content

Preface

This book is for you if you're tired of watching JavaScript struggle with complicated calculations while your users get impatient. I wrote this second edition because WebAssembly 2.0 changes everything, and I wanted to show you exactly how to use it without the usual technical book problems. The first thing we'll do is go through the basics, like memory management and control flow, which are the most important. Then we'll move on to putting together C, C++, Rust, and Python into Wasm modules that actually work. I'll show you how to use multi-threading, profiling and optimisation techniques that I've used in real projects, not just theoretical exercises. I know a lot of you have old Wasm 1.0 code, so I've written a whole chapter about how to move it over without causing any problems.

And we'll also learn how to use WebAssembly in other ways, not just in browsers. You'll learn to work with Dapr for distributed microservices, deploy on Kubernetes, and build cloud-native applications that scale well. There is working code in every chapter that you can use right away. There is no unnecessary information, just practical techniques that solve real problems. I've figured out the tricky parts and the things that can go wrong, and I'm sharing them what actually works. By the time you finish this book, it will have taught you everything you need to build WebAssembly applications so quickly that people will be amazed.

In this book you will learn to:

- Use WebAssembly, manage memory, and control the flow of a program.
- Put together C, C++, Rust, and Python into high-performance WebAssembly modules using Emscripten.
- Build advanced multi-threaded apps using atomic operations, shared memory and thread-safe synchronization patterns.
- Migrate old Wasm 1.0 projects to version 2.0 using proven strategies.
- Combine WebAssembly with Dapr for microservices using patterns for managing data and sending messages.
- Deploy and scale Wasm workloads on Kubernetes clusters with complete control over configuration and secrets management.
- Make performance better by using systematic profiling and advanced compilation techniques for production apps.
- Take care of module imports, exports, and JavaScript interoperability.
- Use tables, memory semantics and dynamic dispatch mechanisms for complex logic.
- Manage networking, security, monitoring, and debugging for WebAssembly cloud-native deployments at scale.

GitforGits

Prerequisites

This book is for programmers who want to put all their applications onto web browsers at the same speed, with the same efficiency and performance. Just knowing the basics of any programming language and how to develop web apps is enough to get through this book.

Codes Usage

Are we in need of some helpful code examples to assist us in the programming and documentation? Look no further! Our book offers a wealth of supplemental material, including code examples and exercises.

Not only is this book here to aid us in getting the job done, but we have our permission to use the example code in the programs and documentation. However, please note that if we are reproducing a significant portion of the code, we do require we to contact us for permission.

But don't worry, using several chunks of code from this book in the program or answering a question by citing our book and quoting example code does not require permission. But if we do choose to give credit, an attribution typically includes the title, author, publisher, and ISBN. For example, "WebAssembly 2.0 Essentials, Second Edition by Emrys Callahan".

If we are unsure whether the intended use of the code examples falls under fair use or the permissions outlined above, please do not hesitate to reach out to us at support@gitforgits.com. We are happy to assist and clarify any concerns.

Acknowledgement

I owe a tremendous debt of gratitude to GitforGits, for their unflagging enthusiasm and wise counsel throughout the entire process of writing this book. Their knowledge and careful editing helped make sure the piece was useful for people of all reading levels and comprehension skills. In addition, I'd like to thank everyone involved in the publishing process for their efforts in making this book a reality. Their efforts, from copyediting to advertising, made the project what it is today.

Finally, I'd like to express my gratitude to everyone who has shown me unconditional love and encouragement throughout my life. Their support was crucial to the completion of this book. I appreciate the help with this endeavour and the continued interest in my career.

Acknowledgement

Chapter 1: Introduction to WebAssembly

In the first chapter, we will look at how the web has evolved and how it's been shaped by historical developments that made people want a more powerful and flexible platform. We'll explore how JavaScript has grown and where it's reached its limits, and we will discover why even the most advanced scripting methods couldn't fulfil the full potential of high-performance web apps. We will get the lowdown on how it all started and how everyone worked together to develop WebAssembly, and we will see the big moments and choices that made it a key web technology. We'll take a really close look at the main design ideas behind WebAssembly, and we will learn how it solves the performance, security and portability problems that have been troubling developers and businesses for a long time.

In this chapter, we will get to grips with the various tools and frameworks, like Binaryen, Emscripten and WABT, that make Wasm development and integration a breeze. We will get a solid understanding of the main concepts and terms, with practical examples to help us along the way. Then we will get to the nitty-gritty of WebAssembly's architecture. We will learn about the principles that make Wasm secure, efficient, and able to adapt to different platforms. By the time we reach the end of this chapter, we will be all set to start building solid, future-proof WebAssembly solutions.

Web before WebAssembly

Long before the introduction of WebAssembly, the web was primarily a medium for sharing documents and static content. In those early days, the developers worked with the basics, like the HTML for structuring pages and CSS for presentation, and with the JavaScript emerging gradually to provide interactive features. While these tools collectively helped deliver visually attractive pages and simple interactivity, they revealed significant limitations as the expectations of both users and developers grew.

The web, in its original form, was not envisioned as a platform for intensive computation, gaming, scientific modeling, or real-time collaboration. As those demands surfaced, browsers began to strain under the weight of user ambition. The developers and organizations repeatedly encountered issues around performance, scalability, portability, and cross-browser compatibility, and all of which placed a ceiling on what could be realistically achieved within traditional web confines. If we think back to the limitations of this era, we will recognize a clear mismatch between the goals of modern app experiences and the inherent design of web technologies.

Rise and Plateau of JavaScript

The introduction of JavaScript was a breakthrough. It enabled a layer of dynamic interactivity previously out of reach for the web. At first, the JavaScript allowed developers to validate forms, respond to user actions, and update page elements in real time. Over several decades, the JavaScript matured through new engines, optimizations, and powerful frameworks such as React, Angular, and Vue. Additionally, the browser vendors invested heavily in engine performance, leading to the rise of V8, SpiderMonkey, and Chakra. Each of these are driving down execution time and increasing the scope of what could run within the browser window. Despite this evolution, we and the peers eventually hit a plateau. While the JavaScript brought impressive flexibility, it was never meant for compute-heavy workloads or complex, memory-intensive operations. The language, being dynamically typed and single-threaded by nature, suffered from inherent performance bottlenecks. There are applications that require audio/video processing, machine learning, or real-time data analytics simply could not match native performance, no matter how advanced the JavaScript became.

And, with growing demands and insufficient capabilities, the industry leaned on browser plug-ins as a workaround. The Adobe Flash, Java Applets, Silverlight, and ActiveX were adopted to bring high performance and broader capabilities to browsers. These plug-ins seemed to satisfy many needs by enabling the execution of compiled code directly in the browser however, the honeymoon period was short-lived. With plug-ins came a host of new problems that we, as a developer or user, could not ignore. The proprietary dependencies created compatibility headaches, and security vulnerabilities became increasingly frequent and severe. As exploit after exploit was uncovered, the browser vendors responded by deprecating and eventually eliminating support for these plug-ins. This marked the end of an era and left many developers back at square one, searching for a secure, performant, and portable alternative.

Native vs. Web

If we were a software engineer experienced with native programming languages like C, C++, or Rust, we would notice an even sharper line drawn between what was possible natively and in the browser. The native applications benefited from nearly unrestricted access to machine resources, strong typing, and predictable performance. However, the porting of these capabilities to the web, was a serious challenge. The computationally demanding workloads were running slow, error-prone, and outright unworkable, especially given the language's loose typing and memory model. The multi-language teams attempting to reuse code or share libraries across platforms were forced to rewrite large portions from scratch or settle for subpar performance. These started undercutting both developer efficiency and business potential in the process.

While browsers grew more powerful, the native applications continued to set the pace for speed, responsiveness, and access to advanced system features. The users naturally gravitated toward experiences that felt immediate and seamless. For business owners and architects, the gap between browser-based and native applications became a roadblock to digital transformation and product evolution. Addressing this split was no trivial matter, as it required bridging the worlds of inherent web safety and portability with the kind of efficiency that only native code had previously delivered.

Case for WebAssembly

The technology of WebAssembly was envisioned as the answer to these persistent challenges and agonizing compromises. It was not designed to replace JavaScript, but to complement it. It brought near-native speed, memory safety, strong security guarantees, and true language diversity to the web platform. We are about to learn how Wasm introduces a low-level, efficient, and portable binary format that can run complex workloads, both inside browsers and beyond. The web platform took its most significant step toward concurrency, high-performance computing, and true cross-platform application universality, and all that was with the introduction of WebAssembly.

Genesis of WebAssembly

To truly grasp the significance of WebAssembly, we need to look at the challenges and the aspirations that drove its inception. The creators of Wasm recognized that the web is too powerful to remain limited by interpreted scripts, yet too widespread to abandon existing standards. Their vision was not simply to add another programming language to browser environments, but to construct a unifying, low-level compilation target that could empower every language, unlock near-native performance, and level up security for real-world applications. The underlying principle driving WebAssembly was always about answering a clear need: **"How can we close the performance and capability gap between native code and what runs on the web?"**

Milestones of WebAssembly

It's not something that happened overnight, but the way WebAssembly has developed can be tracked through a series of deliberate, industry-shaping milestones. We can see Wasm's evolution as a testament to communities and vendors working together to solve complex, universal problems:

Breakthrough in 2015

I'm sure you remember asm.js, Mozilla's experimental JavaScript subset designed to optimise statically-typed, compiled code for the browser. It was a hit, so there was clearly demand for something even faster and more versatile. So, industry leaders from Mozilla, Microsoft, Google, and Apple got together and formed a W3C Community Group, which set a formal collaborative process in motion.

MVP Launch in 2016

The first official WebAssembly browser implementations appeared in Firefox and Chrome, supporting a minimal viable product (MVP) specification. This meant we could finally run C/C++ applications in browsers, and with much better performance than previous workarounds. The developers were pretty happy about this, as Wasm was now a real, vendor-supported standard.

Cross-Browser in 2017

It didn't take long for all the major browsers (Edge, Safari, Chrome, and Firefox) to start supporting WebAssembly natively. The W3C has given the green light to Wasm as a potential web standard, which is a big step in making it a key part of the web's future. At this time, tools like Emscripten and Wasm-bindgen made it easy to turn languages like Rust and C into Wasm modules.

Non-Browser Runtimes in 2019-20

We reached another milestone when the WebAssembly System Interface (WASI) started letting Wasm run outside the browser – on servers, edge nodes and IoT devices – kicking off a new era for app portability. With WASI, we can use Wasm for cloud-native workloads, microservices, and more, making it truly platform-agnostic.

New Features and Languages in 2020-22

It's now got multithreading, support for advanced SIMD operations, and it's more compatible with other languages. Rust and Go could now target Wasm seamlessly, and Wasm became a reliable choice for running sensitive code securely within browsers and enterprise environments. We've seen how Wasm's consistent feature growth has made it a key player in gaming engines, AI inferencing and blockchain clients.

Wasm 2.0 and Ecosystem Maturity

And, most recently, the arrival of Wasm 2.0 marked a significant leap forward: enhancements in performance, richer instruction sets (especially SIMD), advanced concurrency tools, improved bulk memory operations, and more practical multi-value returns. Today, Wasm is woven not just into browsers but into cloud platforms, blockchain projects, and distributed systems through Kubernetes and Dapr integrations.

So, looking at the whole timeline of developments, the best thing about WebAssembly is the way its designers and implementers work together in a collaborative way. They worked with other vendors through W3C, got support from open-source contributors, and got feedback from software engineers all over the world. This helped them keep their priorities balanced between innovation, pragmatism, and long-term sustainability. With every step along the way, the Wasm community has been super reliable, delivering on its promise of making performance predictable, making sure it can be used on any system, and keeping security top-notch. This open vision is becoming more and more important to us, and we're building new Wasm modules, tools and runtimes all the time. From browser performance breakthroughs to broad cross-platform adoption, each Wasm milestone unlocked new possibilities for we as a developer. This progression wasn't accidental. It was the result of continuous, intentional innovation. As we move deeper into this book, we will see how this foundation supports practical Wasm programming, robust integration into the tech stack, and a future where the line between web and native continues to blur.

WebAssembly Design

If we want to understand WebAssembly beyond mere technical details, we need to focus on **why** it's engineered the way it is. The core philosophy behind WebAssembly (Wasm) revolves around three interlocking principles: predictable performance, uncompromising security, and true portability, as explained below:

Predictable Performance

A lot of interpreted scripting languages (like JavaScript) are really flexible, but they're not so great at efficiency for things like image processing, machine learning, or cryptography, which need a lot of computation. Wasm deals with this bottleneck by being a low-level, statically typed binary format. When we compile the code (like C++, Rust or Go) to Wasm, the browser can run it almost as fast as native code because its instructions are a perfect fit for the CPU.

Let's say we need to apply a blur filter to each pixel of a large image in the browser. In JavaScript, processing millions of pixels one after the other would often freeze the user interface or lag behind native implementations. With Wasm, we can turn a C++ blur algorithm into a Wasm module. When you run this in your browser, the code taps directly into efficient memory access and fast arithmetic, letting us process the image smoothly and with near-native speed. This makes once-impractical web tools possible for creative professionals and data scientists. This is predictive performance in action: we don't just hope it will be fast – we can reliably expect it.

Built-In Isolation

Safety is also a big part of Wasm's design. We all know the benefits of sandboxing: Wasm code runs in its own little world, with no access to the user's file system, network, or operating system APIs. This isolation means that even if we run untrusted third-party Wasm, it can't compromise the machine or browser. We can't compromise on strong validation, static typing and enforced memory safety. These choices aren't random; they're the architecture's defence against many of the vulnerabilities that plagued legacy plug-ins or complex JavaScript abuses.

Portability

Before Wasm, we might recall the headaches of porting code across platforms: system differences, browser quirks, and missed optimizations often wasted weeks or months of effort. Wasm's specification is open and platform-agnostic: the same module that runs in Chrome will execute the same way in Firefox, Edge, or even on the server, a blockchain VM, or an edge device. If we compile the business logic as a Wasm module, you're no longer tied to a specific browser engine or even to browsers at all. This opens the door for universal applications, integrated development, and future-proofing the work.

Suppose we create a calculator engine in Rust and compile it to Wasm. We can safely embed this same Wasm module inside websites, desktop apps using Electron, server-side APIs, or IoT platforms. Its logic behaves identically everywhere and neither the security nor performance profile changes with deployment.

All three of these principles are more than just features – they're requirements that build on each other. Improving performance shouldn't weaken security, and making the system more portable shouldn't make it brittle or slow. It's clear that Wasm's strict validation, clear memory model and binary instruction set are great examples of how modern engineering tackles real business and development needs.

WebAssembly and JavaScript

Why WebAssembly Needed?

For years, everyone agreed that JavaScript was the best for client-side programming on the web. All interactive websites, from real-time dashboards to complex single-page applications (SPAs), use JavaScript, and the huge ecosystem of libraries and tools that have developed around it. We could use JavaScript for form validation, AJAX requests, data visualisation and even light gaming, all running straight in the browser. As browsers advanced, JavaScript engines got really powerful. These days, browsers like Chrome's V8, Firefox's SpiderMonkey, and Edge's Chakra have turned them into app platforms. While this helped the web to grow, we and thousands of other developers noticed that JavaScript, despite how flexible it is, has its limits.

We found that JavaScript is convenient, but it's still interpreted (or just-in-time compiled), garbage-collected, and single-threaded. This meant that things like video editing, 3D rendering, scientific simulations, or running legacy codebases written in C++ or Rust were either too slow or just impossible to run efficiently in the browser. Complex applications often had issues being ported well, and it was tricky to get the same performance and features as native platforms. This gap meant we needed a new technology that could run tight code at speeds like native code, and open the web to more languages and tools. That's where WebAssembly comes in.

Duo Power of WebAssembly and JavaScript

Rather than replacing JavaScript, the WebAssembly was designed to work alongside it. We will find these two technologies are **complementary**, each suited to different roles:

- The **JavaScript excels** at dynamic tasks, UI manipulation, event handling, and integrating with browser APIs. It's great for glue code, orchestrating modules, and managing page state.
- The **WebAssembly excels** at performance-critical sections, algorithm-heavy logic, reusable libraries, and migrating legacy modules to the web.

For example, we could build the interactive front-end of a browser-based photo editor in JavaScript while delegating the image processing filters, fast mathematical routines to a WebAssembly module compiled from C++.

Interoperability

The WebAssembly is embedded in the browser's JavaScript environment. We can load, instantiate, and call Wasm modules directly from JavaScript using the WebAssembly API. Also, Wasm modules can communicate with JavaScript using imported and exported functions. This means we can:

- Pass data from JavaScript to Wasm (and back)
- Call a Wasm function for performance-intensive computation
- Use JavaScript to display results, handle UI, or react to user events

There are modern tools like Emscripten or wasm-bindgen simplifies much of this boilerplate. It helps us to focus on architecture and business logic. So, when we get JavaScript and WebAssembly working together, we've got all the flexibility, reach and performance we need for big projects, from browser games to cloud integrations. There's no need to choose one over the other, though. We build hybrid apps where each part uses its strengths, making powerful software for business and entertainment.

As we move on to the next sections, we'll see some real-life examples of this collaboration and find out how to design web apps using both technologies. We'll also discover ways to boost performance that the early web couldn't deliver.

Today's WebAssembly Ecosystem

In the years since its introduction, the WebAssembly ecosystem has evolved into a dynamic, rapidly expanding landscape. Today, we will find Wasm not just at the heart of progressive web applications, but also running in cloud environments, embedded devices, and edge networks. This explosive growth is a testament to the flexibility of Wasm's foundation and to a vibrant open-source community contributing sophisticated tools and frameworks. Together, these elements empower we to build high-performance applications that leverage the best features of the modern web and native platforms alike.

The key to the success of WebAssembly is having mature, interoperable toolchains that make development reliable and productive. Among these tools, **Binaryen, Emscripten, and WABT** stand out as indispensable parts of the WebAssembly toolkit.

Binaryen

The Binaryen is a compiler infrastructure and toolchain library especially focused on optimizing WebAssembly binary and text formats. When we compile the code from C, C++, or Rust to Wasm, the Binaryen makes sure the output is as small, fast, and efficient as possible. For example, we might write complex mathematical logic, and Binaryen will automatically apply optimizations such as dead code elimination and instruction simplification. Advanced users leverage Binaryen for custom tool development, static analysis, and for powering transformations inside other frameworks. As part of the workflow, Binaryen sits between source code and final deployment, ensuring performance and reliability.

Emscripten

The Emscripten is a complete compiler toolchain that lets us port existing C and C++ codebases directly to WebAssembly. When we have native libraries or performance-sensitive application modules written for desktop or server environments, Emscripten is the bridge to the web platform. Not only does it produce efficient Wasm modules, but it also exports JavaScript glue code, allowing seamless integration with web APIs and UIs. For instance, classic games, emulators, and CAD tools have all been successfully ported to run in browsers using Emscripten, thereby showcasing the power of Wasm to close the gap between web and native experiences. The Emscripten also works hand in hand with other tools like Binaryen, chaining advanced optimizations with straightforward application delivery.

WABT

If we want to deeply understand, debug, or manipulate Wasm, WABT gives us the low-level tools we need. WABT provides utilities to convert Wasm binaries to the human-readable WebAssembly Text format (WAT), inspect and modify module internals, and run basic validation checks. As a developer, WABT helps us understand how the code translates into Wasm, troubleshoot modules, and prototype new features or experiments with the Wasm specification itself. For engineering teams building custom compilers or integrating Wasm with unconventional platforms, WABT is frequently an essential diagnostic and learning aid.

Although Wasm was initially targeted by C and C++ compilers, today we can use Rust, Go, .NET (Blazor), AssemblyScript, and even Python and Java to deploy modules to browsers or servers. New languages and runtimes continue to join the ecosystem, bringing an ever-increasing suite of features and developer pathways.

Runtimes, Platforms, Frameworks and Libraries

Everything from browsers like Chrome, Firefox, and Edge to powerful standalone runtimes like Wasmtime, Wasmer, and WasmEdge use WebAssembly to make sure distributed and cloud-native applications are both secure and efficient. They use Wasm in container orchestration platforms (like Kubernetes), at the edge of their networks, or even within blockchain smart contracts and serverless architectures.

There are loads of frameworks that the Wasm ecosystem supports, like Blazor (for .NET), Yew (for Rust), and emscripten-ported SDL or OpenGL stacks. All these libraries mean we can build web UIs and simulation engines and deploy them with both graphical and computational acceleration, without having to worry about the language or platform.

With this move, we will become part of a system where every part – from toolchains like Binaryen, Emscripten, and WABT, to frameworks, languages, and runtime platforms – is designed to boost your productivity, keep things safe, and make things faster. As we get to grips with Wasm, we'll find a world where developers are no longer limited by browser quirks or language silos, but by their imagination and skill.

WASM Core Concepts

In order to really get to grips with WebAssembly, it's vital to understand its fundamentals and the lingo that's used in relation to it. All the different parts of the language, how it's structured, how it's executed and how it's modular, all help to show off Wasm's unique strengths and how it works, especially when we're moving from basic scripting to more complex, scalable applications. We'll break down these concepts, illustrate their roles, and apply them to real scenarios so as to master their **principles** (the WHY) and **applications** (the HOW).

Module

A **module** is the fundamental building block of any WebAssembly application. When we compile code from languages such as C, C++, or Rust, what we generate is a Wasm module typically a **.wasm** binary file. This module is self-contained: it describes its memory, types, functions, and imports/exports. We then load it into a browser or runtime, and it behaves identically no matter where it runs. For example, if we wrote a mathematical library in Rust and compile it to Wasm, we now have a module that we can use both in browser-based apps and server-side compute engines.

Imports and Exports

After a module is loaded, it's instantiated, which means it is prepared for execution and can be provided with specific functions or resources it expects from its host environment (JavaScript or another runtime).

- The **imports** are interfaces through which the Wasm module asks for functionalities not included in itself, such as browser APIs, console logging, or specific data.
- The **exports** are functions, tables, or memory spaces the module provides to the environment, allowing JavaScript or other host code to call into it.

So here, let us say that the module exports an **add** function. So here, the JavaScript in the browser can easily call **add(x, y)**, passing two numbers and getting the result. The imports can be used to provide random number generation, access to external memory, or host-driven callbacks. This is an essential pattern for integrating complex business logic with dynamic web interfaces.

Memory and Linear Memory

Basically, WebAssembly uses something called linear memory, which is a flat, continuous set of bytes that the Wasm code can read and write straight away. All your data, whether it's arrays or strings, is stored in this memory. Unlike with higher-level languages, there's no built-in garbage collector, so we have to manage memory manually and deliberately. Each module can define, use, grow, and (sometimes) share memory across instances. For lots of applications, like graphics, scientific computation, or simulations, it's really important to be able to access linear memory directly for speed and reliability.

Here's an example: If you're building an image manipulation tool, the pixels of the image are stored in linear memory and processed by the Wasm module. Basically, JavaScript interacts by copying data into or out of this memory space, enabling fast, parallel processing of large datasets.

Stack Machine and Execution Model

At its core, the Wasm is a **stack machine**. The instructions are executed in a strict sequence: they push and pop items to/from an internal stack, enabling evaluation of expressions and control flow. This choice of execution model allows the Wasm runtime to optimize code and maintain predictability.

For example, when we write arithmetic or logic in Wasm, you're really stacking up operands and operations. It ensures every calculation is fast, in-order, and safe from out-of-bounds errors.

WAT and .wasm

The wasm modules are distributed as compact, binary files (**.wasm**), making them efficient to download and validate. For development and debugging, we can use the **WAT**, which offers a readable, S-expression-based syntax. There are tools like **WABT** help us convert between WAT and binary, inspect modules, and validate correctness. When we want to understand why a module behaves a certain way, we can inspect and edit its WAT format with WABT, ensuring full transparency into every instruction.

Types and Validation

The WebAssembly uses strong, static typing: every function, memory area, and table entry has a well-defined type that the runtime enforces and validates before execution. This means function calls, memory accesses, and table lookups are all guaranteed to be safe and predictable. For rxample, if we export a function with two integers as arguments and expect one float as a result, the Wasm won't allow us violate this contract. This makes both debugging and optimization easier for we as an engineer.

Tables

The Wasm includes tables, which are basically like arrays, but designed for storing references to functions or objects. This is a bit of avanced stuff, but it's super important when we're working on more complex module patterns, like plug-in systems and dynamic linking.

Host Integration

The WebAssembly interfaces work really well with host environments, mostly with JavaScript via the WebAssembly API, but also with specialised runtimes such as Wasmtime or Wasmer. It's up to us as the developer to provide the module as a binary, load it using the right API, and then interact with host data, events, and resources using imports and exports.

As we move on, we will repeatedly apply these constructs, building everything from toy apps to enterprise-grade systems. Each time we interact with Wasm, these core ideas will guide us in constructing fast, safe, and portable solutions.

Architecture of WebAssembly

And to get the most out of WebAssembly, you've got to understand the thinking behind its core architectural choices. If we get how Wasm works behind the scenes, we will be able to debug, boost performance and get security benefits that we just can't get with traditional web technologies. The architecture is minimalist on purpose, but all the decisions were made to guarantee consistency, safety and high-speed execution, whether you're running it in a browser, on a server or at the network edge.

Stack Machine Model

So, at the heart of WebAssembly is its stack-based virtual machine. Most native CPUs use something called a register-based system, but Wasm is different. Every operation in Wasm works by reading from and writing to a conceptual stack. Say we're doing an addition. The operands get pushed onto the stack, the operation gets done, and the result gets pushed back. This simplicity means we get consistent, portable executables, and the same Wasm binary can run on every compliant engine without modification. The Wasm stack machine model is great for quickly turning code into native instructions, as the stack traces naturally match the function calls and arithmetic stack frames used by modern chips.

Binary Format and Validation

As for wasm modules, they're delivered as compact binary blobs (.wasm). This format is designed to be efficient. It reduces the size of network transfers and lets the browser or runtime validate and parse the module with minimal extra computing power. Before it runs any code, the engine makes sure every instruction is type-safe, memory-safe and determinable. In the past, scripting environments sometimes had bugs or malformed bytecode, but Wasm makes sure that the module follows its strict rules, or it just won't run. This reduces runtime errors and security holes, making it reliable for us and the users.

Memory Model and Safety

The WebAssembly's memory model is built around the concept of linear memory, which is a single, contiguous block of addressable bytes. Unlike native executables, Wasm code cannot access arbitrary device resources or memory outside this block. All reads and writes are bounds-checked, which closes a vast class of bugs and attack vectors endemic to C and C++ programs. We gain peace of mind knowing buffer overflows can't silently corrupt the heap or leak secrets, and all allocations remain within a predictable space. This provides tremendous security benefits for any sensitive or multi-tenant applications we build.

Sandboxing and Host Interaction

It's like a safe box for the code to run in, keeping it all separate and secure. By default, modules can't access the network, filesystem or privileged instructions. Any interactions with the outside, like making API calls, reading files or updating the UI, need to be explicitly provided by the host environment as imports. This model reflects a "deny by default" security posture, meaning you, as a developer or operator, have granular control over which capabilities a Wasm module is allowed to have. Not only does this stop malicious code from exploiting vulnerabilities, but it also makes auditing and compliance a lot easier for regulated industries.

If we want the image processing module to save files, we pass a specific file-write function as an import. If we don't, the module just can't reach storage. You're in charge of the bridge between Wasm and the outside world.

Concurrency and Parallelism

With Wasm 2.0, we can build multi-threaded and highly parallel applications thanks to advanced features like threads, atomic operations, and shared linear memory. These features let us process large datasets, run scientific simulations and use real-time collaborative tools, without having to deal with the limitations of JavaScript's single-threaded nature. This is really useful for business scenarios involving workloads such as AI inference, financial analytics, or streaming media.

Integration and Extensibility

What's great about Wasm's architecture is that it's really easy to fit into all sorts of different environments. From browser engines to edge servers and even databases or blockchain nodes, the embedding API is consistent and minimal. We can deliver portable executables as Wasm modules, and we can be sure that compliant hosts, like Wasmtime, Wasmer, or browser engines, will treat them the same.

Summary

Basically, we took a look at how web development has changed up to the point where WebAssembly came along. We found out about the limitations of the early web technologies and how JavaScript, even though it completely transformed interactive applications, came up against performance and versatility issues for more complex use cases. It traced WebAssembly's origins, charting the key milestones that showed its progress from experimentation to being adopted a lot, and highlighted the collaborative community effort that defined its evolution. It also gave us an understanding of the W3C-backed design philosophy that informed WebAssembly's focus on performance, security, and portability, and showed us practical examples of why these aspects matter in real-world development. It also explained how JavaScript and WebAssembly work together, highlighting their complementary roles and the new possibilities created by efficient interoperation.

We used some key ecosystem components, like Binaryen, Emscripten, and WABT, to show how Wasm development is sped up and made more productive. The chapter then went on to look at the basics of Wasm concepts and terminology, with clear definitions and practical examples, making sure we had a good understanding of the vocabulary for the rest of the book. Finally, by taking a look at the underlying architecture and safety model, we figured out how WebAssembly achieves its consistency, reliability, and security for building future-proof, cross-platform applications.

Chapter 2: Fundamentals of WebAssembly Programming

So, this chapter's going to be all about getting to grips with the crucial elements needed to author, optimise, and execute WebAssembly modules like a pro. First of all, we'll look at how all the bits of a module work together, using both WAT and binary formats to show we what we mean. Then we'll move on to working with data types and variables, building our skills in handling computation and scope effectively. We'll cover control flow techniques next, so we can build programs with predictable and robust logic. There'll be loads of info on how to create, invoke and organise functions, which will get we on the way to writing modular, extensible code.

This chapter's going to show us how to manage linear memory, by showing us how to allocate, initialise, and manipulate it in more complex situations. We're going to get some experience with imports and exports, which'll help us integrate Wasm modules with all sorts of host environments and compose them effectively. We'll be doing some hands-on exercises to show how arithmetic, logic, and structured testing fit together in full programs. By the time we're done, we'll have the skills to design, build, and validate Wasm modules that are perfect for modern web and systems applications.

Understanding WebAssembly Syntax

The WebAssembly modules exist in two main representations:

- A compact binary format (**.wasm**) for execution and distribution, and
- A human-readable text format (**.wat**) for editing, learning, and debugging.

Both the representations and the ability to move between them is must for professional Wasm development.

WAT Writing

The WAT is a structured, parenthesis-based syntax that exposes all module components: functions, types, imports, exports, and memory in a clear, explicit manner. Unlike most high-level languages, the WAT is close to how the WebAssembly virtual machine operates. This transparency makes it valuable for understanding generated modules, performing granular optimizations, or debugging problems that arise from higher-level toolchains.

Following is an example of a simple function written in WAT:

```
(module
  (func $add (param $lhs i32) (param $rhs i32) (result i32)
    local.get $lhs
    local.get $rhs
    i32.add)
  (export "add" (func $add))
```

```
)
```

This module has one function, **add**, that takes two 32-bit integers and gives you their sum. There's no doubt that every aspect of this is spelled out, like the function declaration, parameter types, and export. This makes it easier to learn and understand when you're checking the compiled Wasm.

Working with .wasm Format

When running in the browser or any Wasm-supported runtime, the code must be in the **.wasm** binary format. This form is not meant to be written by hand. Instead, we must write in WAT and then compile to binary.

Now, to convert between formats and inspect binaries, we will use tools such as WABT. The WABT's **wat2wasm** command takes the **.wat** and outputs **.wasm**, while **wasm2wat** lets us convert the binaries back to readable text. For example:

```
wat2wasm add.wat -o add.wasm
wasm2wat add.wasm -o add_out.wat
```

We can write or modify the logic in WAT, compile to a binary, then inspect the output to verify correctness and efficiency. This workflow is especially useful when debugging toolchain output or optimizing modules for deployment.

From WAT to Running Code

First, we write the logic in WAT (add.wat). Then, we compile to binary using WABT or wat2wasm. After this, we load and run the binary using a browser or Node.js environment via the WebAssembly JavaScript APIs.

Following is a basic JavaScript snippet showing how to load and use the module:

```
const fs = require("fs");
const wasmBuffer = fs.readFileSync("add.wasm");
WebAssembly.instantiate(wasmBuffer).then(obj => {
  const result = obj.instance.exports.add(5, 3);
  console.log("Sum:", result); // Outputs: Sum: 8
});
```

This gives us complete clarity and control over the Wasm modules. We can see the details in WAT, control the output in binary, and bind it to the applications. This provides both, understanding at the source level and optimal integration into production workflows.

Working with WebAssembly Data Types

The WebAssembly makes sure that you can always predict how it will run, which reduces runtime errors. The data types defined by the WebAssembly specification are short and sweet, making them both speedy and easy to use on the go. It's really important to understand how to use these data types in practice, and by expanding on the previous add function example, we can see exactly how each type works in a real module workflow.

Numeric Types

The WebAssembly provides four primary numeric types:

- **i32**: 32-bit integer
- **i64**: 64-bit integer
- **f32**: 32-bit floating point
- **f64**: 64-bit floating point

Each of the above type is tailored for specific computational needs, from simple counting to advanced scientific calculations. When building functions, we declare parameter and return types explicitly, ensuring the module is tightly optimized for the task.

Integer Addition (i32)

We can modify the initial **add** function to illustrate various data types in action. Start with integer addition (as before), then introduce floating point addition and demonstrate how multi-type operations work:

```
(module
  (func $add (param $lhs i32) (param $rhs i32) (result i32)
    local.get $lhs
    local.get $rhs
    i32.add)
  (export "add" (func $add))
)
```

This function expects and returns 32-bit integers, suitable for basic arithmetic and counting operations.

Floating Point Addition (f32)

```
(module
```

```
  (func $add_float (param $lhs f32) (param $rhs f32) (result
f32)
    local.get $lhs
    local.get $rhs
    f32.add)
  (export "add_float" (func $add_float))
)
```

This shows how WebAssembly can handle real numbers accurately. We would use this for graphics processing, scientific modeling, or financial calculations.

64-bit Types

For advanced needs, we can use **i64** for large integers (like timestamps or cryptographic keys) or **f64** for high-precision math.

```
(module
  (func $add_long (param $lhs i64) (param $rhs i64) (result
i64)
    local.get $lhs
    local.get $rhs
    i64.add)
  (export "add_long" (func $add_long))
  (func $add_double (param $lhs f64) (param $rhs f64) (result
f64)
    local.get $lhs
    local.get $rhs
    f64.add)
  (export "add_double" (func $add_double))
)
```

We may also make use of these types for algorithms needing extensive computation, cryptography, or scientific simulation.

Variables and Scope

The Variables are essential for managing data throughout program execution, and understanding how they are declared, used, and scoped is crucial for building efficient and maintainable Wasm modules. The WebAssembly organizes variables into two main types; one is **local variables** and the other is **global variables**. Each of them are with distinct scope behaviors and lifetimes.

Local Variables

The local variables are declared inside functions using the **local** keyword and are confined to the scope of the function in which they reside. Their scope means these variables exist and can be accessed **only** while the function is running. As soon as the function call completes, all locals are discarded, and their values are lost. This behavior protects against unintended side effects and makes local variables ideal for temporary computations within a function.

For example, let us revist the **add** function with a local variable in the following program:

```
(module
  (func $add_with_local (param $lhs i32) (param $rhs i32)
(result i32)
    (local $sum i32) ;; Declare local variable
    local.get $lhs
    local.get $rhs
    i32.add
    local.set $sum ;; Store result in local variable
    local.get $sum) ;; Retrieve and return local variable
value
  (export "add_with_local" (func $add_with_local))
)
```

In the above, the **$sum** is only accessible within **$add_with_local**. If we try to access the **$sum** outside this function, it will result in a compilation error as its scope doesn't extend beyond the function boundary.

Furthermore, the local variables follow the concept of **lexical scope**, meaning that nested blocks or loops inside a function can also declare their own locals, but these inner locals are not visible outside their block. This enables us to write well-structured and modular Wasm code without variable name collisions or accidental overwrites.

Global Variables

The global variables have a broader scope. They are declared at the module level and persist for the lifetime of the module instance. Unlike locals, globals are accessible by any function within the module, enabling shared state or configuration data across multiple invocations.

The globals can be **immutable** or **mutable**:

- Immutable globals are constants and cannot be changed after module instantiation.
- Mutable globals allow read and write access from functions, meaning their values can change during execution.

Following is a quick example of a mutable global maintaining a running total:

```
(module
  (global $running_total (mut i32) (i32.const 0)) ;; Mutable
global initialized to 0
  (func $add_to_total (param $val i32) (result i32)
    global.get $running_total
    local.get $val
    i32.add
    global.set $running_total
    global.get $running_total)
  (export "add_to_total" (func $add_to_total))
)
```

In the above, we can see that the **$running_total** retains its value between calls, and thus it provides persistent state accessible throughout the module.

The scope of local variables is function-limited, and its lifetime is during function execution only. Each time a function is called, locals are freshly initialized, preventing data leakage across calls. On the other hand, the **global variables scope is module-wide, lifetime spans the entire module instantiation.** It support persistent state and are shared across functions. This clean separation of scope prevents accidental interference across code sections and enforces a modular design where small, reusable functions can trust their local state without unintended side effects.

Control Flow and Structured Programming

What happens to the instructions in a program is determined by the control flow. This decides whether they're executed sequentially, conditionally, or repeatedly. WebAssembly has got structured control flow that's both easy to predict and performant, using explicit constructs that you'll recognise from other low-level languages. It's also designed to offer robust safety and optimisation potential.

Sequential Execution and Blocks

Every function in WebAssembly executes its instructions in order unless directed otherwise by branching or looping constructs. To group instructions or establish new scopes, we use **blocks**:

```
(block $my_block
  ;; Instructions inside the block execute in sequence
)
```

A block can contain any number of instructions, and it also creates a new scope for variables declared within it.

Conditional Logic

The decision-making is supported with the **if** and optional **else** constructs. Each structure evaluates a condition (a value left on the stack) and executes the relevant branch:

```
(module
  (func $compare (param $a i32) (param $b i32) (result i32)
    local.get $a
    local.get $b
    i32.gt_s ;; Is $a > $b?
    if (result i32)
      i32.const 1 ;; true branch: a > b
    else
      i32.const 0 ;; false branch: a <= b
    end)
  (export "compare" (func $compare))
)
```

This function returns **1** if the first argument is greater than the second, otherwise **0**. The **if** block evaluates the comparison result and chooses the appropriate branch. It leverages the structured flow to prevent hidden side effects.

Loops

The WebAssembly's **loop** construct implements repetitions, similar to low-level **while** or **for** loops. The block re-executes by branching to its start with a **br** (break) instruction.

Following is a quick example on creating a decrementing loop:

```
(module
  (func $countdown (param $start i32) (result i32)
    (local $i i32)
    local.get $start
    local.set $i
    block $exit
      loop $repeat
        local.get $i
        i32.const 1
        i32.sub
        local.tee $i ;; update and keep value
        i32.const 0
        i32.gt_s
        br_if $repeat ;; Branch to start if $i > 0
      end
    end
    local.get $i)
  (export "countdown" (func $countdown))
)
```

In the above, we set **$i** to **start** and decrements it, looping until **$i** reaches zero. The **br_if** checks if the loop should continue, showcasing precise flow control in Wasm.

Branching

The **BR label** will always exit a block or jump to another part of the code. If the value on the stack is non-zero, then **br_if $label** will jump conditionally. The **br_table** offers multi-way branching based on an index value, similar to using a switch statement in C or Java. All these constructs are great for implementing structured, non-linear flows within WebAssembly modules. They help us to avoid the unpredictable jumps of legacy low-level code, making our program logic more advanced.

By combining **if**, **loop**, and branching, we can build complex decision trees, iterative calculations, and responsive, high-performance modules.

Defining and Using Functions

The functions are a key part of WebAssembly, working as the basic building blocks for efficient, reusable and modular computation. Each function has its own set of clear parameters and return types, making things clearer and allowing for better optimisation. If you know how to define, invoke, and connect functions, you'll be able to build maintainable and high-performance Wasm modules.

Function Signatures and Parameters

A function signature in WebAssembly describes the parameter types and the return type. We declare a function using the **func** keyword, specifying parameters and the type returned. Functions support multiple parameters and, in Wasm 2.0, can return multiple values. Each parameter is strongly typed, so we must match the expected types exactly at every invocation.

Let us work upon the earlier numeric example having a module with two related functions:

```
(module
  (func $add (param $x i32) (param $y i32) (result i32)
    local.get $x
    local.get $y
    i32.add)
  (func $add_and_double (param $a i32) (param $b i32) (result
i32)
    call $add       ;; Call the previously defined $add
function
    i32.const 2
    i32.mul         ;; Double the result
```

```
    )
  (export "add" (func $add))
  (export "add_and_double" (func $add_and_double))
)
```

In this example, the **$add_and_double** demonstrates calling one function from another, passing the parameters **$a** and **$b** to **$add**, and then multiplying the result by two for further calculation. This modular pattern allows we to decompose complex logic into smaller, testable parts.

Multiple Return Values

With Wasm 2.0, the functions can now return several values. It enables functions to produce richer outputs without workarounds. Following is a function returning both the sum and difference of two numbers:

```
(func $sum_and_diff (param $x i32) (param $y i32) (result i32
i32)
  local.get $x
  local.get $y
  i32.add                    ;; first result: sum
  local.get $x
  local.get $y
  i32.sub                    ;; second result: difference
)
(export "sum_and_diff" (func $sum_and_diff))
```

In the above, when we call **sum_and_diff**, both results are returned as a tuple, and can be accessed in the host environment.

Invoking Functions from JavaScript

The WebAssembly functions are invoked from JavaScript through the module's exports. After instantiating the module, each exported Wasm function can be called just like a regular JavaScript function.

Following is a quick example on invoking the functions:

```
const fs = require("fs");
const bytes = fs.readFileSync("the_module.wasm");
```

```
WebAssembly.instantiate(bytes).then(obj => {
  console.log(obj.instance.exports.add(5, 3));          //
Outputs: 8
  console.log(obj.instance.exports.add_and_double(5, 3)); //
Outputs: 16
});
```

This whole pattern makes Wasm powerful for sharing logic between web frontends, server processes, and even hardware edge deployments.

Efficient Memory Management

The memory handling is central to enabling rich applications, high-speed computation, and seamless integration with the outside world. Unlike many high-level languages, the wasm offers direct, fine-grained control over memory, and focusing upon performance and explicit access.

Linear Memory

The WebAssembly provides a single, contiguous space known as **linear memory**, which is conceptually similar to a resizable array of bytes. Every module can declare and manage this linear memory explicitly, and all data including the numbers, objects, images, strings must be stored inside it.

Let us see in the following about a module initializing the memory with the **memory** definition:

```
(module
  (memory $mem 1) ;; Declare one memory page (64 KiB per page)
)
```

In the above, the additional pages can be allocated dynamically with **memory.grow** when more space is needed, and thereby providing flexibility as the application handles growing workloads or large datasets.

Working with Data Segments

The data stored in linear memory must be initialized carefully. The wasm uses **data segments** to load static values upon module start. For example, we can preload an array of bytes for later computation as shown in the below:

```
(module
```

```
  (memory 1)
  (data (i32.const 0) "\01\02\03\04") ;; 4 bytes at offset 0
)
```

Then the functions can read or write these bytes directly. We build some pretty powerful memory-aware modules by combining this ability with arithmetic or data processing routines.

Access and Manipulation

The WebAssembly instructions such as **i32.load, i32.store, i64.load**, and their floating-point counterparts enable direct access to and from linear memory. These instructions require an offset (address) and operate on 4 or 8 bytes at a time. For example, in the following, we will incorporate the memory access into a function which is related to earlier arithmetic example:

```
(module
  (memory (export "memory") 1)
  (func $sum_from_memory (param $ptr i32) (result i32)
    ;; Sum the two 32-bit integers stored at offsets ptr and
ptr+4
    local.get $ptr
    i32.load
    local.get $ptr
    i32.const 4
    i32.add
    i32.load
    i32.add)
  (export "sum_from_memory" (func $sum_from_memory))
)
```

In the above, the function expects a pointer to a memory location where two integers are stored. It reads them using **i32.load**, sums the values, and returns the result.

Memory Interaction from JavaScript

In practice, the memory is a bridge. The JavaScript can allocate an **ArrayBuffer**, write values, and share it with Wasm. After loading the module, we can write to Wasm memory and invoke exported functions:

```
const fs = require("fs");
const bytes = fs.readFileSync("memory_module.wasm");
WebAssembly.instantiate(bytes).then(obj => {
  const memory = obj.instance.exports.memory;
  const view = new Uint32Array(memory.buffer);
  view[0] = 10;   // First 32-bit int
  view[1] = 32;   // Second 32-bit int
  console.log(obj.instance.exports.sum_from_memory(0)); //
Outputs: 42
});
```

We can control every stage of this process, from the declaration to the initialisation, dynamic growth, and reading and writing, using both Wasm and host code. And that means we can manage data really precisely. All of this is really important for building graphics tools, numerical analysis utilities, cross-language integrations, and more, making memory-conscious programming a professional cornerstone in WebAssembly development.

Imports, Exports, and Instantiation

The modules form the organizational backbone of WebAssembly. Each module can define its own functions, memory, tables, and global variables, and can also interact with other modules or host environments by importing and exporting features. This modular thing makes it easier for we to break down complex applications, share libraries, and integrate Wasm seamlessly into larger systems.

Exports

To use any WebAssembly function, memory, or value in JavaScript or another host, we declare it as an export. For instance, in earlier arithmetic examples, a module explicitly exported **add** and **add_and_double**, making these functions accessible to the outside world:

```
(module
  (func $add (param $x i32) (param $y i32) (result i32)
    local.get $x
    local.get $y
    i32.add)
```

```
  (export "add" (func $add))
)
```

When JavaScript loads this module, **add** is available as an immediate callable function, enabling interactive business logic, UI updates, or data processing in web or Node environments.

Imports

The modules can also declare imports, allowing them to leverage functionality from the host (often JavaScript) or from other Wasm modules. The common imports include math utilities, random number generators, or system calls that are unavailable inside the Wasm sandbox by default.

Following is a module that imports a logging function from the environment:

```
(module
  (import "env" "log" (func $log (param i32)))
  (func $increment_and_log (param $val i32) (result i32)
    local.get $val
    i32.const 1
    i32.add
    tee_local $result ;; Store result for both logging and
returning
    call $log
    )
  (export "increment_and_log" (func $increment_and_log))
)
```

In the above example, the function receives a value, increments it, logs the result via the imported **$log** function, and then returns the new value. The import declaration makes it possible for the host app to inject its own functionality into Wasm's deterministic execution.

Instantiating Wasm Modules

After compiling and exporting a Wasm binary, we instantiate it in the application. The instantiation means loading the module, preparing its memory, and wiring up all imports and exports. Now here, the JavaScript provides the **WebAssembly.instantiate** API for this purpose. So here, for imports, we can supply an object containing the required host functions:

```
const importObject = {
  env: {
    log: (x) => console.log("Result:", x)
  }
};
const fs = require('fs');
const buffer = fs.readFileSync('module.wasm');
WebAssembly.instantiate(buffer, importObject).then(obj => {
  obj.instance.exports.increment_and_log(5); // Logs: Result:
6
});
```

In this, we have control over which features are exposed, ensuring robust encapsulation and modular reuse. The functions and memory can be exported individually, or we can expose entire collections for more complex applications.

Arithmetic and Logical Operations

The arithmetic and logic operations are at the core of nearly every computational task, empowering WebAssembly modules to perform calculations, determine conditions, and transform data efficiently. Now here, the wasm provides a comprehensive set of operations that operate directly on its numeric data types, allowing the code to run with predictable performance across platforms.

Arithmetic Operations

For each numeric type (**i32, i64, f32, f64**), Wasm offers familiar arithmetic instructions:

- Addition: **i32.add**, **f64.add**, etc.
- Subtraction: **i32.sub**, **f32.sub**, etc.
- Multiplication: **i32.mul**, **f64.mul**, etc.
- Division: Both signed and unsigned for integers: **i32.div_s**, **i32.div_u**, **f32.div** for floats.
- Remainder (modulo): **i32.rem_s**, **i64.rem_u**, etc.

Here, we can apply these instructions by working directly with the stack. For example, a multiplication function for 32-bit integers appears as:

```
(func $multiply (param $a i32) (param $b i32) (result i32)
```

```
  local.get $a
  local.get $b
  i32.mul)
(export "multiply" (func $multiply))
```

This above compact logic means Wasm routines for math-heavy tasks are concise and map extremely closely to native processor instructions.

Logical Operations

The wasm includes bitwise and logical instructions vital for masking flags, implementing checksums, and optimizing data manipulation:

- AND: i32.and
- OR: i32.or
- XOR: i32.xor
- NOT (bitwise complement): i32.eqz (compare with zero), or combinations for bit manipulation

For example, a simple bitwise AND function would look like:

```
(func $bitwise_and (param $x i32) (param $y i32) (result i32)
  local.get $x
  local.get $y
  i32.and)
(export "bitwise_and" (func $bitwise_and))
```

Both these allow us to compare values and directly support writing conditions in more advanced logic:

- Equal: i32.eq, f64.eq
- Not Equal: i32.ne
- Less than: i32.lt_s, f32.lt
- Greater than: i32.gt_s, f32.gt
- Less/Greater or Equal: i32.le_s, i32.ge_s, etc.

For example, we can check if both the two integers are equal:

```
(func $is_equal (param $a i32) (param $b i32) (result i32)
  local.get $a
  local.get $b
```

```
  i32.eq)
(export "is_equal" (func $is_equal))
```

It'll return **1** if it's equal, **0** if not.

These low-level operations are the foundation for all kinds of algorithms, whether they're scientific, cryptographic, graphical or business logic. The instructions it uses are small, and they're written in a way that makes sure the calculations are fast and stable in any environment it supports. With these tools, we can create much more complex functions, providing clear, consistent results to higher-order modules and modern web applications.

Composing and Testing a Simple Wasm Program

So, building a complete WebAssembly program means going from writing the module in WAT to running and validating its behaviour within a runtime like Node.js. The key to keeping things smooth in this workflow is seeing each step as all linked up – like the source being written, compiled, and executed as one big connected module.

To get started, you'll want to design the module in WAT. So, let's say we're after a module that can do addition and multiplication, so we can use those in other environments.

```
(module
  (func $add (param $x i32) (param $y i32) (result i32)
    local.get $x
    local.get $y
    i32.add)
  (func $multiply (param $a i32) (param $b i32) (result i32)
    local.get $a
    local.get $b
    i32.mul)
  (export "add" (func $add))
  (export "multiply" (func $multiply))
)
```

This above text format defines a program where two mathematical functions (**add**, **multiply**) are available for external use. These functions are exported, ensuring other systems can invoke them directly.

Next, we then compile this text module to the binary format required by WebAssembly environments. For this, we can make use of a tool like WABT to convert:

```
wat2wasm math.wat -o math.wasm
```

After this, we now have a binary program, **math.wasm**, which contains both the arithmetic functions, structured for efficient loading and execution.

The program is consumed by a runtime. In Node.js, load the binary, instantiate it, and access the module's exports just as we defined them. This integration step maintains the exact structure and function signatures as written in the WAT source:

```
const fs = require('fs');
const buffer = fs.readFileSync('math.wasm');
WebAssembly.instantiate(buffer).then(obj => {
  const { add, multiply } = obj.instance.exports;
  const resultAdd = add(10, 20); // computes addition in Wasm
  const resultMultiply = multiply(6, 7); // computes
multiplication in Wasm
  console.log('Add 10 + 20:', resultAdd);
  console.log('Multiply 6 * 7:', resultMultiply);
});
```

This above sequence mirrors exactly what we defined. The numbers sent to **add** and **multiply** become operands within the Wasm module, get processed instantly, and the result is returned to the environment. We can test further by altering input or exporting additional functionality.

Summary

So, to sum up this chapter, we looked at how WAT and binary formats work, and how they affect the module's behaviour from the moment it's defined to when it's executed. We explored numeric and advanced data types, and this showed us how important it is to manage types precisely and think about performance. We also talked about how to manage variables, focusing on scope and lifetime, and how locals and globals work together in actual computations. Basics like blocks, conditionals and loops were broken down to show how they help to structure and predict a program. We used function definitions, including multi-parameter and multi-value returns, to show how the code is organised in modules.

Then the chapter moved on to memory management, giving us ways to declare, set up and use linear memory in real-life situations. It showed how modules work with hosts and keep things encapsulated. We also looked at a bunch of different arithmetic and logical instructions to help us work with data more easily. At last, a full WebAssembly program was created and tested, bringing all concepts together in a connected workflow from source to runtime.

Chapter 3: WebAssembly Modules and Semantics

In this chapter, we're going to take a look at some essential intermediate skills for building efficient and flexible WebAssembly modules. We'll get to grips with all the fancy semantic stuff when it comes to tables, like how they store function references, make dynamic calls possible, and support code architectures like plugin management and command routing. We'll also go into a lot of detail about linear memory, showing we practical ways to build, index and process arrays or objects by manually managing memory offsets. This gives us the power to work with custom data layouts. We'll find ways to link WebAssembly logic to event-driven application architectures, and see how hosts like browsers or backend servers trigger Wasm code in response to user actions, messages, or system signals.

We'll be focusing on concurrency, so we'll be looking at how Wasm modules handle memory sharing between threads safely, and how atomic instructions make sure everything runs smoothly across multiple threads. We'll be linking each concept to some practical examples, so we will see how the workflows look in action when it comes to simulation, analytics, and microservices. When we're finished, we'll be able to design, develop and optimise Wasm modules that use dynamic code execution, handle data well, react to events, and make the most of parallel computing power.

Advanced Table and Memory Semantics

The **tables** in WebAssembly are similar to arrays, but they are designed to hold references to functions (and in Wasm 2.0, other reference types). It enables **indirect function calls**, which is handy for creating dynamic logic such as function dispatch tables, plug-in architectures, or polymorphic behaviors. We can generally define a table at the module level, specifying size and type (typically **`funcref`** for storing function pointers).

Table Basics

Let us say that we want dynamic dispatch of two arithmetic operations (add and multiply). So here, we start by placing their references in a table:

```
(module
  (table 2 funcref) ;; Table with 2 slots for functions
  (func $add (param i32 i32) (result i32)
    local.get 0
    local.get 1
    i32.add)
  (func $multiply (param i32 i32) (result i32)
    local.get 0
    local.get 1
```

```
    i32.mul)
  (elem (i32.const 0) $add $multiply) ;; Fill table
)
```

This sets up a table with references to **$add** and **$multiply**, enabling calls through an index rather than direct calls.

Indirect Calls & Dynamic Dispatch

The tables become powerful when we want code to decide at runtime which function to call. And, this is done using **call_indirect**, which takes a signature index (function type) and table index, executing the referenced function:

```
(type $math (func (param i32 i32) (result i32)))
(module
  (type (func (param i32 i32) (result i32)))
  (table 2 funcref)
  (func $add (param i32 i32) (result i32)
    local.get 0
    local.get 1
    i32.add)
  (func $multiply (param i32 i32) (result i32)
    local.get 0
    local.get 1
    i32.mul)
  (elem (i32.const 0) $add $multiply)
  (func $dispatch (param i32 i32 i32) (result i32)
    local.get 1
    local.get 2
    local.get 0
    call_indirect (type 0))
  (export "dispatch" (func $dispatch))
)
```

The **$dispatch** function takes a table index and two operands. It chooses either **$add** or **$multiply** based on the index and calls the function indirectly. This dynamic dispatch approach is essential for patterns like plugin systems, polymorphism, or command routing in large applications.

Linear Memory Semantics

Earlier, the linear memory was introduced as a contiguous resizable byte array. Its advanced usage includes managing complex data, such as arrays, structs, strings. We can allocate space, write values at specific offsets, and use load/store instructions to manipulate them:

```
(module
  (memory 1)
  (func $store_two_values (param $ptr i32) (param i32) (param
i32)
    local.get $ptr
    local.get 1
    i32.store
    local.get $ptr
    i32.const 4
    i32.add
    local.get 2
    i32.store)
  (export "store_two_values" (func $store_two_values))
)
```

In the above, the function stores two 32-bit integers in linear memory at a given pointer. The handling of strings or objects involves encoding and managing offsets carefully.

In advanced Wasm applications, the tables and memory are frequently used together: tables for indirect function calls and dynamic dispatch, linear memory for fast, structured data storage. The synergy enables we to design interpreters, plugin hosts, or event-driven systems that scale and evolve efficiently.

Complex Data Structures

The WebAssembly's linear memory and tables allow us to manage arrays and dynamically call functions. We can try to simplify these ideas by breaking each process into concrete, approachable steps as shown further.

Storing and Reading Integers

Let us consider that we want to store two 32-bit integers in memory and read them back. Here, we will use a pointer that marks where to start writing:

```
(module
  (memory (export "memory") 1)
  (func $store_two_numbers (param $ptr i32) (param $first i32)
(param $second i32)
    local.get $ptr
    local.get $first
    i32.store           ;; Store $first at $ptr
    local.get $ptr
    i32.const 4
    i32.add
    local.get $second
    i32.store)          ;; Store $second at $ptr+4
  (export "store_two_numbers" (func $store_two_numbers))
)
```

This above function accepts a memory pointer and two values, storing them side by side. The first integer goes to the base address, and the second goes 4 bytes further (since **i32** uses 4 bytes).

Summing a Small Array

Next, to sum an array, we will loop through each value by stepping through memory:

```
(func $sum_two_numbers (param $ptr i32) (result i32)
  local.get $ptr
  i32.load                  ;; Load first number
  local.get $ptr
```

```
    i32.const 4
    i32.add
    i32.load                ;; Load second number
    i32.add                 ;; Sum them
)
(export "sum_two_numbers" (func $sum_two_numbers))
```

This function loads the two integers (from the same memory locations as before) and returns their sum.

Using Table for Dynamic Function Calls

The tables let us switch which function to run at runtime. For example:

```
(table 2 funcref)
(func $add (param i32 i32) (result i32)
  local.get 0
  local.get 1
  i32.add)
(func $multiply (param i32 i32) (result i32)
  local.get 0
  local.get 1
  i32.mul)
(elem (i32.const 0) $add $multiply)
(func $dispatch (param $which i32) (param $x i32) (param $y
i32) (result i32)
  local.get $x
  local.get $y
  local.get $which    ;; Index in the table: 0 for add, 1 for
multiply
  call_indirect (type 0))
(export "dispatch" (func $dispatch))
```

With this, we can call either add or multiply by passing 0 or 1 as **$which** respectively to **$dispatch**.

So just to sum up, we split the logic by writing a function for each step, like one to store values, one to process (like summing), and one to choose operations dynamically. It makes the WebAssembly code easier to build, more readable, and reliable.

Event-Driven Programming and Host Integration

The event-driven architectures are built around a specific idea. And the idea is that the code reacts to events such as, user actions, network requests, timers, or messages from other systems. In a traditional browser or server setting, there are events that might come from button clicks, API responses, or socket signals. And, to support event-driven programming with WebAssembly, we then rely on the host environment (JavaScript in a browser) to detect and forward events to WebAssembly modules for fast, predictable processing.

Conceptually, the WebAssembly itself does not generate or manage events. Instead, the Wasm code is designed to react when the host invokes an exported function as a response to some event. For example, we might export a function called **onButtonClick**, and have JavaScript call this function whenever a user clicks a button. This arrangement is the key. The JavaScript listens for events, and hands control to WebAssembly functions that process the event payload and return results or side-effects. This pattern is universal, as it is used for UI interactivity, handling API data, orchestrating microservices, and more. We can link multiple event handlers by exporting several functions tailored to each possible event type.

Integrating Wasm with JavaScript Events

Let us say that we want a WebAssembly module to process numbers whenever a browser button is clicked. So here, we define an exported Wasm function that expects input:

```
(module
  (func $process (param $val i32) (result i32)
    local.get $val
    i32.const 2
    i32.mul) ;; Doubles the input number
  (export "process" (func $process))
)
```

Once compiled to **.wasm**, use the following JavaScript to connect an HTML button click to the Wasm processor:

```
const fs = require('fs');
const buffer = fs.readFileSync('process.wasm');
WebAssembly.instantiate(buffer).then(obj => {

document.getElementById('myButton').addEventListener('click',
() => {
    const input =
parseInt(document.getElementById('numInput').value, 10);
    const result = obj.instance.exports.process(input);
    document.getElementById('output').textContent = 'Result: '
+ result;
  });
});
```

Every time the button is clicked, the host collects the value, passes it into the WebAssembly function, and displays the result.

This pattern is not limited to UI events. We can use similar techniques in server-side platforms or microservices. If a node receives a new message, HTTP request, or timer tick, it invokes a Wasm function with the event data. This enables using WebAssembly for fast business logic, analytics, or validation in response to any external trigger for large systems.

WebAssembly Threads and Concurrency

Multithreading transforms what WebAssembly can deliver, allowing modules to run code in parallel and unlock performance for everything from scientific computing to interactive games. Supporting concurrency requires a clear understanding of how threads work with shared memory, atomic operations, and the host environment.

Threads, Shared Memory, and Safe Parallelism

Traditionally, early WebAssembly modules ran in a single thread, like every function call, memory access, and computation occurred within one continuous execution flow. The complex apps, however, often need to perform multiple actions at once. For example, we might want to update graphics, fetch data, and process input all at the same time. With threads, the WebAssembly lets us run several routines in parallel. Achieving safe parallel execution starts with declaring a shared memory. This shared memory is a fixed region of linear memory that multiple threads, such as browser workers or server worker threads, can access at the same time. The magic is in synchronization: without it, threads could overwrite each other's changes or corrupt information, creating hard-to-debug errors. To prevent this, WebAssembly provides atomic operations that ensure updates to shared memory happen in a consistent, lock-safe manner. Every atomic load or store is guaranteed not to be interrupted, keeping data reliable no matter how many processors are involved. This design mimics proven concurrency models found in lower-level languages such as C++ and Rust. We can control exactly when and how threads modify shared state, making programs predictable and robust.

Setting up Shared Memory

The threads cannot function without a properly declared shared memory region. In WebAssembly, the shared memory must be explicitly specified during module definition. We can assign the **shared** flag in the memory declaration and set minimum and maximum page counts.

Let us see a sample of it:

```
(module
  (memory (export "memory") 2 20 shared)
)
```

As you can see, the module creates an exported shared memory block, which is initially sized at two pages (128 KB, as one page equals 64 KB) and expandable up to twenty. The host environment, like a browser, will use this memory buffer to let multiple workers access the same data. Passing memory references between workers lets threads work together on processing, storing results, or updating state without duplicating content. If you get the sizing right, you're all set. If you've got a bigger workload or a lot of data, you'll need more pages, but if it's a smaller job, you'll use less.

Atomic Operations and Synchronization

The thing is, we can only be sure that shared memory across threads is handled properly if we use atomic instructions for every variable that can be changed at the same time. There are a few atomic instructions in WebAssembly that cover load, store, and read-modify-write for integer types. These operations stop race conditions, where two threads might otherwise read, change, or save values at the same time, which can lead to unpredictable outcomes. Like, if you want to increment a counter safely across threads, you'd use **i32.atomic.rmw.add**.

```
(func $increment_counter (param $off i32)
  local.get $off
```

```
  i32.atomic.rmw.add 1 ;; Add 1, atomically, to integer at
offset
  drop)
(export "increment_counter" (func $increment_counter))
```

From the above program, when the threads call this function, the atomic instruction ensures only one thread updates the value at a time, so no increments are lost. There are other atomic operations such as, compare-and-swap, or atomic stores that allows for robust custom synchronization schemes, including flags, queues, and locks.

Running Threads

The WebAssembly threads do not start themselves; the host is responsible for launching and coordinating parallel computation. In browsers, the **SharedArrayBuffer** API allows the main thread to create a buffer and transfer it to multiple workers, each running a Wasm instance. Each worker receives the shared memory and can call Wasm export functions, performing tasks such as incrementing counters, updating grids, or processing chunks of data. A typical integration involves loading the Wasm module in each worker, sharing the memory object, and passing relevant byte offsets or values as function arguments. The worker threads can post messages back to the main thread, communicating when they finish or if results need to be aggregated. Server-side environments like Node.js use similar patterns, leveraging built-in worker threads for creating parallel pipelines and sharing memory for big data or analytics workloads.

Summary

In this chapter, we took a close look at advanced WebAssembly tables and linear memory. We took a look at some previous arithmetic examples and then moved on to practical steps for storing, reading and manipulating numeric arrays in linear memory. So, it had clear breakdowns of functions for handling multiple integers and for performing dynamic function dispatch using table indices. It was really important to talk about how to manage arrays and represent complex data structures using offset calculations.

We also talked about event-driven programming, explaining how external environments like browsers or servers can forward events to exported Wasm functions, so we can react straight away to external triggers. The hosting model, where JavaScript or other environments detect events and invoke specific Wasm logic, was shown to be both flexible and broadly applicable beyond UI interactivity. The chapter focused on WebAssembly threads and safe concurrency, showing how shared memory and atomic operations let several routines run and safely update data at the same time.

Chapter 4: Bridging WebAssembly with High-Level Languages

In this chapter, we're going to find out how to add powerful multi-language support and streamlined interoperability to our WebAssembly projects. The first thing we'll do is get to grips with putting together and moving C, C++, Rust, Java and Python programs over to Wasm. There'll be loads of helpful tips on how to get the tools set up, the environment sorted, and how to do the best compilation on Linux. We're going to take a dive into how Emscripten, wasm-bindgen, TeaVM, Pyodide, and related toolkits make porting a breeze, opening up old and high-performance code to the web. Basically, we'll be looking at how to integrate Wasm modules with JavaScript, focusing on passing data, invoking exported functions, and working with glue code to connect computation with the DOM.

There'll be different ways to swap arrays, strings and objects between Wasm and JS so we can make more complex apps. We'll take a close look at how Rust, Java, Python and Wasm work together in real-world projects, using communication layers to make it all happen. By doing this, we'll get better at modular architecture, stateless function composition, profiling, and dividing responsibilities in a smart way.

Fundamentals of Compiling and Porting to WebAssembly

When you take code written in high-level languages and bring it over to WebAssembly, you basically translate or compile the source files into the portable, efficient .wasm binary format. This means we can run tried-and-tested, but previously limited, code in browsers, cloud services and other host environments. This extends the reach and versatility of the logic.

Core Toolchains

The **C and C++** rely heavily on **Emscripten**. It is a well-established toolchain that leverages the LLVM backend to output WebAssembly modules directly from native code. The **Rust** features first-class Wasm support in its build tools, using the **`wasm-bindgen`** system to expose functions and handle type translation. The **Java** developers use **TeaVM**, which compiles Java bytecode into Wasm, and the **Python** users can employ **Pyodide** to precompile interpreter and packages for browser-based analytics and scripting. Each of these languages also has its own runtime or glue code to help integrate Wasm modules with web APIs, system features, and data exchange.

Compiling and Porting

So for porting code to Wasm, the usual workflow goes something like this:

Choose and Setup the Toolchain

First, you need to pick a Wasm-capable compiler or framework that suits the language. Then you can install and configure Emscripten for C/C++, set up Rust's toolchain for Wasm, or prepare TeaVM or Pyodide for Java or Python. Also, make sure the development environment is ready for Wasm compilation, ideally on Linux or another supported platform.

Adapt Source Code

Then, get the code ready for Wasm by getting rid of any operations that aren't supported, like direct file system access or native threads, unless you're targeting WASI or hosts that have threading enabled. It's best to focus on logic and algorithms that don't rely on OS-specific features and can be used on any platform.

Compile Source

After adapting the source code, you then run the compiler or build tool to produce the **`.wasm`** file, and, if needed, make use of the JavaScript glue code for integration with web environments. The Emscripten can output both Wasm modules and a JS harness, while the Rust's toolchain can generate bindings for direct JavaScript interoperability.

Validate and Iterate

And then you can load the output Wasm file in a browser, Node.js, or a Wasm runtime. The idea is to test how well it actually works and how quickly it performs, making sure you get the right results and that it's efficient. We'll polish the code, tweak the compiler settings, and keep going until we've got a solid port.

Ecosystem Tools and Future Directions

Since then, we've got some new tools like **`AssemblyScript`** (for TypeScript-to-Wasm), **`wasm-bindgen`** (for Rust), and **`WABi`** (a universal binding toolkit), which has made Wasm much more useful. They make it easy to quickly try out new ideas, make it so different languages can work together more smoothly, and improve how well things work on a variety of technology stacks. The more we do, the better we'll get at picking, setting up and tweaking these tools for WebAssembly projects of all sizes. We'll be able to turn desktop, scientific or custom business logic into modules that'll run safely on any platform that supports Wasm.

Up and Running with Emscripten

We use Emscripten to compile C and C++ projects to WebAssembly, which means we can run binaries efficiently in browsers and other Wasm environments. First, we'll install it and get everything ready, then it's time to actually compile and optimise the source programs.

Installation and Configuration

Install System Dependencies

On a Linux system, we first update the package listings and install Python, CMake, Git, and build-essential packages:

```
sudo apt-get update
sudo apt-get install -y python3 cmake git build-essential
```

These tools are prerequisites for managing Emscripten's compiler infrastructure and source builds.

Setup Emscripten SDK

Then just clone the Emscripten SDK repository, initialise it and activate the latest compiler set:

```
git clone https://github.com/emscripten-core/emsdk.git
cd emsdk
./emsdk install latest
./emsdk activate latest
source ./emsdk_env.sh
```

This process downloads the latest SDK, compiler tools, and configures shell environment variables (**`PATH`**, **`EMSDK`**, etc.) so the Emscripten commands are available globally.

Validate Configuration

After this, we then check the availability using:

```
emcc -v
```

This prints the Emscripten version and confirms a working installation.

Compiling, Running, and Optimizing C++ Program

Suppose we have a simple C++ source (**`calc.cpp`**) for addition and multiplication:

```
extern "C" {
  int add(int x, int y) { return x + y; }
  int multiply(int x, int y) { return x * y; }
}
```

Compile to Wasm

We then run the following:

```
emcc calc.cpp -O3 -s WASM=1 -s
EXPORTED_FUNCTIONS="['_add','_multiply']" -o calc.js
```

This above command then compiles with high optimization (**-O3**). It ensures WebAssembly output (**-s WASM=1**). It also specifies function exports for host usage and produces both **calc.wasm** and a JavaScript loader (**calc.js**) for easy integration

Run and Test

In a browser, link the generated files and call exports after instantiating the module. In Node.js, we can use the following script:

```
const fs = require('fs');
const { add, multiply } = require('./calc.js');
console.log('Add:', add(5, 7));          // Outputs 12
console.log('Multiply:', multiply(6, 3)); // Outputs 18
```

The Emscripten supports multiple optimization flags (**-O2**, **-Oz** for size optimization), dead code elimination, and link-time optimizations. We can adjust compilation flags to shrink output size or boost performance according to deployment target, and use **emcc --help** for advanced options. Overall, a well-configured Emscripten toolchain and hands-on compilation workflow bring the C and C++ source code to Wasm with efficient exports, runtime integration, and performance tuning for production applications.

Integrating WebAssembly with JavaScript

Once we are done with compiling our code to Wasm, we then import the binary into JavaScript. And, for this, we make use of the standard WebAssembly API. So here, let us consider that we want the Wasm module to export two functions, **add** and **multiply**. For this, we will load and invoke them as in the below sample code:

```
const fs = require('fs');
const buffer = fs.readFileSync('calc.wasm');
WebAssembly.instantiate(buffer).then(({ instance }) => {
  console.log(instance.exports.add(8, 7));         // prints
15
```

```
  console.log(instance.exports.multiply(3, 4));     // prints
12
});
```

In the above, we are passing integers directly to Wasm and getting results back in JavaScript.

Now, there come situations when we want our Wasm module to call a JavaScript function, maybe for updating the DOM or logging output. To achieve this, we first define the import in Wasm (using Emscripten or raw WAT) and then supply the implementation in JavaScript.

So here, let us say that our Wasm expects a function called **updateDom**:

```
(module
  (import "host" "updateDom" (func $updateDom (param i32)))
  (func (export "sendToDom")
    i32.const 123
    call $updateDom)
)
```

And in our JavaScript, we then implement it as follows:

```
const importObject = {
  host: {
    updateDom: x =>
document.getElementById('result').textContent = `Result: ${x}`
  }
};
WebAssembly.instantiate(buffer, importObject).then(({ instance
}) => {
  instance.exports.sendToDom();
});
```

Now, in the above, each time **sendToDom** is called in Wasm, the result updates an element on the web page.

Let us move on to exchanging more complex data, like arrays and strings. For arrays, we typically take advantage of shared memory. Suppose our Wasm exports a block of memory; in JavaScript, we use a typed array to set values and then pass a pointer into Wasm:

```
const memoryBuffer = instance.exports.memory.buffer;
const typedArray = new Float64Array(memoryBuffer, 0, 10);
typedArray.set([2.25, 3.5, 4.0, ...]);
const result = instance.exports.sumArray(0, 10); // Assuming
Wasm export
document.getElementById('output').textContent = `Sum:
${result}`;
```

In the above, our sum is computed inside Wasm and the result appears in the DOM.

When it comes to strings, we need to encode them. In JavaScript, we use **`TextEncoder`** before placing them in Wasm memory, and **`TextDecoder`** for reading back. We copy the bytes into memory and hand pointers to our Wasm functions:

```
const encoder = new TextEncoder();
const stringBytes = encoder.encode('Hello WebAssembly!');
const mem = new Uint8Array(instance.exports.memory.buffer);
mem.set(stringBytes, strPtr); // strPtr points to memory
location
instance.exports.processString(strPtr, stringBytes.length);
// To read output, use TextDecoder
```

For objects, we flatten or serialize them, either as arrays or strings, before passing over. Let us say we pack an object as **`[id, value]`** in memory and then let Wasm process it.

When we want Wasm logic to react after a user event, we write JavaScript glue code that hooks into the DOM and calls Wasm exports. For example, consider doubling a number entered by the user:

```
document.getElementById('doubleBtn').onclick = () => {
  const num = parseInt(document.getElementById('input').value,
10);
  const doubled = instance.exports.multiply(num, 2);
  document.getElementById('result').textContent = `Doubled:
${doubled}`;
};
```

In the above, the JavaScript reads the value, sends it to Wasm, and then updates the DOM.

Multi-Language Support and Wasm Bindings

In modern WebAssembly development, we are not limited to just C or C++. We can bring in other high-level languages such as Rust, Java, and Python, and make them interact smoothly with Wasm modules. The key is understanding how bindings connect data and functions between Wasm and the host language.

Integrating Rust

Let us look at how we get a Rust function to run as WebAssembly and communicate with JavaScript. We first write a Rust function we want to compile:

```
#[no_mangle]
pub extern fn triple(x: i32) -> i32 {
    x * 3
}
```

We then build this to Wasm using the Rust toolchain:

```
cargo build --target wasm32-unknown-unknown --release
```

The output **`.wasm`** file exports the **`triple`** function. Now, using **`wasm-bindgen`**, we can generate the necessary JavaScript glue so we can call **`triple`** directly from JS:

```
wasm-bindgen target/wasm32-unknown-
unknown/release/the_crate.wasm --out-dir ./out
```

We then import and use it in JS:

```
import init, { triple } from './out/the_crate.js';
await init();
console.log(triple(7)); // prints 21
```

We have now successfully connected Rust and JS using efficient Wasm bindings.

Integrating Java using TeaVM

If we are working in Java, we use TeaVM to compile Java bytecode to Wasm. Suppose we have this Java code:

```
public class MathOps {
    public static int doubleValue(int val) {
        return val * 2;
    }
}
```

After compiling with TeaVM, the resulting **.wasm** makes the methods available for JS to invoke exports, following similar patterns as before. Practical interaction requires JS code that loads and calls the module's functions with suitable arguments, handling memory management as necessary.

Python via Pyodide

So with Pyodide, we can run Python code that's been compiled to Wasm in the browser. It puts Python code together with the interpreter and all the things it needs to run. In JS, we load Pyodide and then run Python code strings, or call WASM-compiled Python functions straight away:

```
let pyodide = await loadPyodide();
let result = await pyodide.runPythonAsync('sum([3, 5, 8])');
console.log(result); // prints 16
```

Now, Python logic runs side-by-side with JS and can return results to JS for further use in the web app.

Wasm Bindings for Robust Integration

The bindings like **wasm-bindgen** for Rust, the bridge mechanisms in TeaVM for Java, and Python wrappers in Pyodide allow us to:

- Export and call pure functions
- Share data types across boundaries
- Manage memory automatically for high-level code

These frameworks help us avoid manual serialization and make multi-language integration much easier, especially when dealing with arrays, strings, and even objects.

Language Interoperability Best Practices

And when we're working on strong hybrid applications with WebAssembly, we're not just connecting code, we're building systems that are easy to maintain, fast and clear. The first thing to remember is that it's really important to divide logic up carefully so that performance-critical routines, numeric calculations and heavy batch processing are all put into Wasm modules, while UI logic, event handling and communication with broader frameworks go into JavaScript or the main host.

Before we exchange data, we analyze requirements. We pass primitive types like numbers directly, rely on typed arrays for bulk transfer (such as **`Int32Array`**), and always encode/serialize strings and objects, typically using UTF-8 and structured arrays. The strings use **`TextEncoder`** for JS → Wasm and **`TextDecoder`** for Wasm → JS. Whenever we have objects with multiple fields, we break them into flat buffers before sending to Wasm.

For maintainability, we want our Wasm modules to be stateless and pure whenever possible. The pure functions, those that only use their arguments are easier to compose and test. If we need persistent state, we use globals with great caution, making sure all state mutations are tracked clearly and documented. For applications where many calls might happen in parallel, we avoid mutable module-level state, instead sending explicit state as arguments or via dedicated memory regions.

To make maintenance and upgrades simple, we keep interoperability modular: Wasm code is in clear modules with exports; JS glue code is kept in its own file; interfaces are documented. We version our exports, use test scripts for every change, and track function signatures so new contributors (or future us) can extend our application without facing hidden issues. Now, let us see how these practices work in a production-like snippet.

Suppose we want to sum an array of integers in Wasm and update the UI from JS:

- Pure Array Processing

```
extern "C" {
    int sum_array(int* data, int len) {
        int sum = 0;
        for (int i = 0; i < len; ++i) sum += data[i];
        return sum;
    }
}
```

We have no global state and always pass buffers and lengths as stateless, fast, and easy to test.

- Efficient Data Handling and DOM Integration

```
const numbers = [7, 12, 5, 3];
```

```
const { memory, sum_array } = instance.exports;
const buf = new Int32Array(memory.buffer, 0, numbers.length);
buf.set(numbers);
const sum = sum_array(0, numbers.length);
document.getElementById('sumResult').textContent = `Sum:
${sum}`;
```

In the above, we lay out all our logic: memory is efficiently exchanged, computation is clearly marked, and UI is updated in JS only. This code is readable, easy to extend, and robust if called repeatedly or in parallel.

Summary

To sum up the learnings form this chapter, we understood the practical aspects of compiling and porting C, C++, Rust, Java, and Python to WebAssembly using Emscripten, wasm-bindgen, TeaVM, and Pyodide. We learned to setup and config Emscripten, after which sample C++ programs were efficiently compiled, run, and optimized for Wasm execution. We then learned to integrate WebAssembly modules with JavaScript through exports, imports, and glue code for DOM operations and event handling. Various techniques for direct and complex data exchange involving arrays, strings, and objects between Wasm and JS were demonstrated.

The chapter also provided extensive coverage to multi-language bindings, and we reviewed approaches for sharing data structures and passing function calls across language boundaries. We also explore some of the best practices across making use of stateless Wasm functions, typed arrays, modular glue logic, performance profiling, and maintaining clean separation between computation and UI.

CHAPTER 5: ADVANCED WEBASSEMBLY TOOLS AND TECHNIQUES

This chapter is all about getting used to the various strategies and technical workflow required to optimize WebAssembly modules for real-world deployment. In this, we will start by exploring the problem of unoptimized Wasm binaries and the impact of excess code and slow performance. We will then set up Binaryen and integrate it with the existing build and compiler toolchains for repeatable results. Through hands-on missions and real code samples, we learn to inspect, run, and measure key optimization passes using Binaryen command-line tools.

Nex,t we will see some of the optimization techniques, like dead code elimination, loop unrolling, inlining, and constant folding. We will explore benchmarking and validation methods to analyze and confirm the effects of the optimization. The chapter then aims to turn into a Wasm engineer who can routinely deliver modules that load fast and run lean, ready for the demands of modern browsers, networks, and users.

Getting Binaryen Ready

I'll give you an example. There's a user on a slow mobile connection trying to load our site. Every byte matters, so if your code is bigger, there'll be longer waits, more data charges and potential lost users. When the performance is poor on mission-critical dashboards or interactive UIs, people get frustrated and leave.

As Wasm engineers, our goal is to create modules that download quickly, run efficiently, and deliver the intended experience regardless of device or bandwidth. We're on the lookout for ways to cut the excess, polish the performance, and give us more control over what ships. That's where Binaryen comes in. So, it's about time we turned our Wasm binaries, which are pretty rich but a bit wild, into simple, professional-grade modules. That way, they'll be ready for real products and users who expect the best.

Installing Binaryen

Now that we understand why optimization truly matters for Wasm modules, let us begin by installing Binaryen on our system. The easiest way is to use **git** to clone the source, then build it:

```
# First, get the source code
git clone https://github.com/WebAssembly/binaryen.git
cd binaryen
# Now, build Binaryen tools
cmake . && make
```

When the build is complete, we will find binaries (like **wasm-opt**, **wasm-dis**, **wasm-as**) inside the **bin/** directory.

And, to make sure everything works, let's quickly check:

```
./bin/wasm-opt --version
```

From the above, we should see the current Binaryen version, confirming we are ready to optimize Wasm modules.

Integrating with Emscripten Build

If we are using Emscripten to compile our C or C++ to WebAssembly (as we learned earlier), Binaryen actually fits perfectly into this workflow. Emscripten can invoke Binaryen tools automatically for us, but it's good to know how to use them manually for more control.

Let us say we compile a program called **`calc.cpp`**:

```
emcc calc.cpp -O3 -s WASM=1 -o calc.wasm
```

After this, we run Binaryen manually for further optimization:

```
./bin/wasm-opt calc.wasm -O4 -o calc-opt.wasm
```

This thing gives us a highly optimized, production-ready binary. We can make this a regular step, wherein it is wired into our build scripts or the automated CI pipelines.

Implementing Optimization

Now that we have Binaryen set up and integrated with our compiler toolchain, let us put it to work with a real WebAssembly binary. Let us consider that we have compiled a C++ program called **`matrix.cpp`** that performs matrix multiplication, which is quite a common compute-heavy scenario familiar in simulations, graphics, or data processing. So here, we will try to optimize this Wasm module step-by-step using Binaryen tools and see how each pass improves size and speed.

- Inspecting Raw Module

First, we will understand the contents of our original binary. We can use **`wasm-dis`** to disassemble it into WAT format:

```
./bin/wasm-dis matrix.wasm -o matrix.wat
```

After this, we then open the **`matrix.wat`**, in which we see the function definitions, memory usage, and imports/exports. This transparency lets us verify generated code and spot large or redundant segments.

- Applying Basic Optimization

Next, we then apply the first round of optimizations with Binaryen's **wasm-opt**:

```
./bin/wasm-opt matrix.wasm -O1 -o matrix_opt1.wasm
```

This performs simple optimizations like removing unused local variables and dead code. We can track the file size and performance benchmarks pre- and post-optimization to measure gains.

- Aggressive Optimization Passes

Next, we then run a deeper optimization and it is very easy as shown below:

```
./bin/wasm-opt matrix.wasm -O3 -o matrix_opt3.wasm
```

The **-O3** enables advanced compiler passes: function inlining, loop unrolling, constant folding, and more. It can significantly speed execution but require careful testing to avoid subtle bugs.

We can also disassemble the optimized modules again and then can use the diff tools to compare against the original. And after this, we then script these optimization steps into our build pipeline. Every commit triggers Wasm build and optimization, generating small, fast binaries ready for deployment.

Through this, we see the Binaryen as a vital collaborator that helps us polish, secure, and improve WebAssembly code in every stage of professional development.

Day-to-Day Wasm Engineering Best Practices

Now that we have optimized our **matrix.wasm** binary using Binaryen, let's dig deeper into the specific optimization techniques and see how they impact our project in a realistic setting. By focusing on this example, we will observe how changes to optimization flags and strategies affect both binary size and runtime performance.

Using Optimization Levels

First, we recall that we started with a basic module compiled from **matrix.cpp**. Now here initially, we might have used a straightforward command:

```
emcc matrix.cpp -O1 -s WASM=1 -o matrix.wasm
```

In the above, the **-O1** gives us basic optimization, but Binaryen lets us push further. The testing shows that as we raise the optimization level using **wasm-opt**, the resulting **.wasm** file typically shrinks and can run faster.

Let us take the following sample code:

```
./bin/wasm-opt matrix.wasm -O2 -o matrix_O2.wasm
```

```
./bin/wasm-opt matrix.wasm -O4 -o matrix_O4.wasm
```

With the above, we then measure and compare these files. The higher the **-O** flag, the more thorough the optimizations.

Measuring Effects

Now after each optimization, we can run commands like:

```
ls -lh matrix.wasm matrix_O2.wasm matrix_O4.wasm
```

It helps to check the size changes, and then benchmark execution (in Node.js or browser) for speed:

```
console.time('matrix');
instance.exports.matrix_multiply();
console.timeEnd('matrix');
```

Very oftenly, we observe size dropping by 10–30% and run time getting noticeably faster. For matrix-type programs, this can mean a big improvement in app responsiveness.

In production, we default them to **-O3** or **-O4** during our CI/CD pipeline. However, we always validate outputs, as sometimes aggressive optimization can break edge cases or make debugging harder. For critical releases, we keep both unoptimized and optimized **.wasm** files for comparison, regression testing, or debugging after deployment.

Summary

Overall, we learned to face the challenges of real WebAssembly projects that require practical optimization for performance and size. We learned why raw Wasm module builds are often suboptimal for production use, with unnecessary code and slower load times impacting user experience. And, then with setting up the Binaryen, we successfully established a reliable workflow for Wasm optimization. We then optimized a sample matrix multiplication module to apply, inspect, and validate optimization passes such as dead code elimination, constant folding, and inlining.

The chapter also showed us how increasing the optimization levels directly improved file size and runtime speed. We also measured these results and learned to automate them within our build pipelines for continuous performance improvement. Throughout this chapter, we saw how professional Wasm engineers use Binaryen to deliver robust, efficient modules ready for deployment, setting both technical and workflow standards for sustainable WebAssembly development.

CHAPTER 6: ADVANCED PERFORMANCE OPTIMIZATION

In this chapter, we will dive into the essential techniques and strategies of WebAssembly performance engineering. At first, we will get into the core dimensions of Wasm performance, including startup time, raw execution speed, and resource efficiency across browsers and devices. Next, we will engage with hands-on profiling and benchmarking. For this, we will use JavaScript timers, browser Performance panels, and code-level instrumentation to identify and fix bottlenecks. We will next explore memory management thoroughly to minimize allocations and avoid fragmentation for scalable workloads.

Next, the chapter will introduce multithreading and concurrency, teaching we how to split heavy computation and leverage parallel hardware in both browsers and server-side Wasm deployments. We will then master advanced optimization through lazy loading, feature code splitting, and staged module initialization for seamless user experiences. And finally, we will learn to deploy Wasm efficiently, in which we will combine browser caching, CDN best practices, server pooling, release automation, and version rollback for resilient, high-speed distribution. With all these techniques getting mastered, we will be equipped to build Wasm applications that outperform expectations for all users, anywhere.

WebAssembly Performance Fundamentals

Once we begin building real-world WebAssembly modules, performance quickly moves from being a theoretical concern to a frontline reality that shapes user experience and technical success. If we or the team deploy a Wasm-powered web dashboard, graphics engine, or data-intensive service, we will start encountering real performance expectations from users and stakeholders. The difference between a module that loads and runs "just okay" and one that responds instantly can mean the difference between user engagement and abandonment, reliable analytics or missed opportunities, and scalable business growth or technical debt.

We will now get into the foundational performance concepts every Wasm engineer should know right from the planning phase.

Startup Latency

Latency is basically how long it takes for the WebAssembly module to be downloaded, decoded, compiled, and instantiated by the browser or host environment before it can start executing functions. And this is really important for apps that are used by people, because you only have a short amount of time to make a good impression. For example, loading a dashboard, rendering the first animation frame, or completing a login verification is sensitive to this initial time.

There are several factors that contribute to startup latency:

- **Network Speed**

The **`.wasm`** file must be transferred over the internet. File size and compression (gzip, Brotli) matter. Even small improvements add up, especially on mobile networks.

- **Browser Decoding and Compilation**

The browsers must parse, validate, and compile Wasm binaries to native machine code. The efficiency of this step varies with browser and device because the Chrome uses TurboFan, V8; Firefox leverages SpiderMonkey; Safari employs JavaScriptCore. Each engine has strategies and tradeoffs.

The good news is that there are some pretty cool tricks engineers use to get things going faster, like code splitting (loading only the modules you need), lazy initialization, using streaming compilation APIs, and optimising the binary using toolchains like Binaryen.

Runtime Throughput and Execution Speed

Once the Wasm module is loaded, the true performance story begins in how fast and efficiently code runs. Throughput includes raw computation speed, memory access patterns, and how many function calls can be made under real load. If you're running Monte Carlo simulations or real-time signal processing, every millisecond counts.

There are several aspects that shapes the throughput:

- The first is the **algorithm choice.** It is an highly tuned algorithms (matrix multiplication, sorting, DSP) dramatically affect run time. The Wasm supports near-native speed, if we use optimized C/C++/Rust code as input.
- The next is the **Wasm-JS Boundary Cost.** The thing is, calling functions back and forth between JS and Wasm can create overhead. If you batch process and don't do too many cross-boundary calls, you'll see a speed boost.
- And, there is **Parallelism.** The modern Wasm allows multithreading, and thereby speeding up workloads like video rendering, machine learning inference, or heavy data crunching.

In practice, we measure throughput using microbenchmarks (run many iterations and average result) and real-world testing (with actual user inputs and varying data sizes).

Resource Usage

The performance isn't just about speed. It is an efficient resource usage that ensures the module doesn't slow or crash the browser, leak memory, or hog system power. The WebAssembly exposes a contiguous block of linear memory. We are responsible for allocation, freeing, and avoiding fragmentation.

There are some key strategies exists which includes:

- **Pre-allocating Memory** in which we reserve enough memory at startup, such that we grow only when needed.
- **Smart Data Layouts** are structure arrays and objects for cache-friendly access patterns.
- And, there is another trick, called **Memory Profiling.** In this, we use the browser devtools, Emscripten's heap profiler, and custom logging to track allocation and spot

leaks.

Cross-Browser and Cross-Device Variability

The Wasm aims to be portable, but each browser's implementation has quirks, and different devices (ARM, Intel, mobile, desktop) show unique behaviors. The performance tuning requires cross-platform benchmarking, using tools to compare module speed on Chrome, Firefox, Edge, and Safari. Today, WebAssembly engines are rapidly evolving. Occasionally, the optimizations specific to one engine (say, V8 in Chrome) can influence design decisions.

In my opinion, I want to recommend some of the best practices, like:

- Make sure you test on the main browsers and devices, not just on the development machine.
- Try to use portable, standards-compliant code wherever you can. If it's not absolutely critical, avoid browser-specific hacks.
- Keep on top of the latest Wasm engine releases and community benchmarks.

As we take ourselves forward into our Wasm projects, we can at the leat set one goal, which is to **optimize for every stage**, right from the download and initialization to raw computation and memory management, across browsers and hardware.

Profiling and Benchmarking WebAssembly

When we start thinking about real-world performance, the first thing to do is to profile and benchmark our WebAssembly modules. Profiling means measuring where time and resources are being spent, and benchmarking means running repeatable tests so we know how fast our code is actually running, not just guessing or relying on intuition. In the following section, we'll go through some practical techniques, the tools we use, example measurements, and how to take our analysis to the next level beyond basic timing.

Instrumentation and Tools

First, we decide what to measure. Usually, it's how long it takes to run specific Wasm functions (like "matrix_multiply" or "process_image") and how much memory is used before and after those runs. The best way to do this is to combine the tools that are already built into your browser with some lightweight JavaScript instrumentation. So, in the following, we load our Wasm module via Emscripten for a realistic test scenario, and we instrument our calls:

```
console.time('matrix');
instance.exports.matrix_multiply();
console.timeEnd('matrix'); // Prints e.g. 'matrix: 27.42ms'
```

In the above, we can see a real elapsed time, including JS→Wasm overhead. For more repeatable results, we can run the computation many times and average the times like in the following program:

```
function benchmarkMatrix(iterations) {
  const start = performance.now();
  let dummy = 0;
  for (let i = 0; i < iterations; i++) {
    dummy += instance.exports.matrix_multiply();
  }
  const end = performance.now();
  const avg = (end - start) / iterations;
  console.log(`Average matrix_multiply time: ${avg} ms`);
}
benchmarkMatrix(1000);
```

This gives us a much better sense of everyday performance, smoothing out one-off slow spikes or background events.

Using Chrome DevTools and Flame Graphs

Let's get more advanced. Just open Chrome, load the Wasm project, and open DevTools (Ctrl+Shift+I). Then switch to the "Performance" tab and hit Record, doing the benchmark or clicking through UI actions that trigger Wasm functions. When we stop recording, have a look at the flame graph: colourful stacks show time spent per process, including inside Wasm (often labelled as "wasm-function" or with source map names if enabled).

If we zoom in on these segments, we can spot which routine is using up cycles. We keep an eye out for JS→Wasm boundary overhead (lots of small calls might be slower than a big, batched call). When it comes to tight compute loops, long bars are the way to go – they're like the ultimate optimisation targets. If our module is multithreaded (using Web Workers with shared memory), we can profile the main thread and workers separately, and see how parallelism impacts runtime.

Tracking Memory Usage and Detecting Leaks

First, switch to the "Memory" or "Performance" tab and take heap snapshots before and after running critical Wasm routines. The DevTools will reveal allocations and objects per execution. However, if a big spike persists after the benchmark completes, we might have a memory leak often shown by growing "ArrayBuffer" or "Wasm Memory" segments that never drop.

When memory allocation is part of the Wasm logic (malloc/free, manual buffers), Emscripten or wasm-bindgen can help us insert logs; for example, we can simply print the **`Module._get_free_memory()`** or similar hooks to monitor heap status from JS.

Node.js Benchmarking and Automated Testing

The profiling isn't just for browsers. If we're running Wasm on Node.js, we rely on **`performance.now()`** (built-in), plus external module profilers like **`clinic.js`** or **`benchmark.js`**. To achieve the robust pipelines, we can automate benchmarks as below:

```
const { performance } = require('perf_hooks');
function runBenchmark() {
  const start = performance.now();
  instance.exports.simulate();
  const end = performance.now();
  return end - start;
}
console.log(`Simulation took: ${runBenchmark()} ms`);
```

In this, we can then add the regression checks to ensure the performance doesn't degrade after each commit, thereby treating timing metrics as critical as correctness itself. By combining code instrumentation, browser profiler analysis, memory management tracking, and repeatable benchmarks, we are able to truly understand our WebAssembly module under real conditions, setting the stage for targeted, high-impact optimization in the rest of our engineering workflow.

Hands-On Profiling

We now learn to carry out a detailed benchmark and profiling session using the sample matrix multiplication program **`matrix_multiply`** we have already discussed. Here, our goal is to turn this practical function into a performance case study, capturing real measurement data, analyzing the results, and iterating improvements based on what we find.

Setting up Benchmark Environment

To begin with, we first make sure the WebAssembly module is compiled and exported properly. With the help of Emscripten, we begin to compile our C++ matrix code:

```
emcc matrix.cpp -O3 -s WASM=1 -s
EXPORTED_FUNCTIONS="['_matrix_multiply']" -o matrix.js
```

After this, we then load the module in a standard HTML/JS application or a Node.js environment. For browser testing, we want a simple interface to trigger the computation and log timings:

```
<button id="runMatrix">Run Matrix Multiply</button>

<div id="output"></div>

<script src="matrix.js"></script>

<script>

Module.onRuntimeInitialized = function() {

  document.getElementById('runMatrix').onclick = function() {

    console.time('matrixMultiply');

    let result = Module._matrix_multiply(); // The function
must be exposed as _matrix_multiply

    console.timeEnd('matrixMultiply');

    document.getElementById('output').textContent = 'Result: '
+ result;

  };

};

</script>
```

Running Benchmark Multiple Times

To obtain the reliable numbers, we need to run the benchmark in a loop and average timings in JavaScript as below:

```
function benchmark(iterations) {

  const times = [];

  for(let i=0; i<iterations; i++) {

    const t0 = performance.now();

    Module._matrix_multiply();

    const t1 = performance.now();
```

```
    times.push(t1-t0);
  }
  const average = times.reduce((a,b)=>a+b,0)/times.length;
  document.getElementById('output').textContent = `Average
Time: ${average.toFixed(3)} ms`;
}
benchmark(1000); // Run 1000 iterations for a good sample size
```

This loop smooths out slow spikes and gives us a clear baseline for both optimization and regression testing.

And for bigger projects, it's a good idea to save scripts and timing output for every major release. Set up automated benchmarks in CI/CD to spot regressions and check performance over time. And as we keep working on this, our matrix multiplication module will get better and better, and it'll be super fast.

Fine-Tuning Memory

At production scale, the management of memory isn't just about avoiding crashes. It's about performance, stability, and long-term reliability. The WebAssembly modules use a contiguous block of linear memory, exposed to both Wasm and JavaScript for allocation and manipulation. If you don't manage your memory properly, you might find your computer's performance is slow, your browser is unstable and you can't easily track down bugs. So, let's have a look at and try out the key techniques for minimising allocations, avoiding fragmentation, and tuning linear memory for the best results.

Minimizing Allocations

The simplest and most effective memory optimization is to reduce the frequency and size of allocations. Every time the Wasm code requests new memory from an internal heap or via **`malloc`**, there is always the overhead. So here, if we allocate and release memory often within tight computational loops, the browser engines may struggle to reclaim resources quickly. It will slow down the execution and potentially causing the memory to swell.

So here, the solution is to pre-allocate buffers that are reused for many calculations. For example, instead of allocating temporary arrays during each matrix multiplication, allocate them once and overwrite values for each new calculation:

```
static int tempResult[MAX_SIZE]; // Allocate once
void matrix_multiply(int* a, int* b, int n) {
```

```
    // Overwrite tempResult each time, no new allocation
}
```

In JavaScript, when passing buffers into Wasm, use long-lived **TypedArray** views over the module's exported memory, rather than recreating them for each call.

Avoiding Fragmentation

When there are lots of small allocations and deallocations, they leave the heap with scattered, unusable spaces, which makes it more likely that there'll be out-of-memory errors and slowdowns. There's a bigger chance of this happening in interactive or server-heavy Wasm apps that run for ages or handle different workloads.

There are two ways to go about it here:

- One of the things we're keen on is putting our money into a few big investments rather than loads of small ones. Whenever you can, do your batch work so you can group allocations. For example, allocate entire rows or columns of a matrix at once instead of individually.
- The other thing you can do is use pool allocators or freelists for recurring data structures. This way, you can reuse freed memory quickly without having to do repeated searches.

For C/C++ modules compiled with Emscripten, we can employ the custom allocator implementations (such as **tlsf** or **jemalloc**) for pool management.

Tuning Linear Memory

The best way to design Wasm programs is to get the right memory configuration. If memory is too small, you'll get frequent **grow_memory** calls, and each one causes slow reallocation. If it's too big, we end up wasting bandwidth and device resources when it's loading.

We can get around this issue by looking at how much work there is and setting realistic limits on the memory. For example, you can pre-allocate based on the largest expected data set (like the upper bound for matrix operations):

```
(memory $mem 1 20) ; Start with 1 page (64KB), allow up to 20
pages
```

And we can keep an eye on how much memory is being used and only add more when we really need to. We can use browser DevTools, Emscripten's HEAPU8.length or Wasm memory API to see how it's used in the real world. If the workload has regular phases (startup, peak usage, idle), we can think about using dynamic resizing logic to manage allocation proactively. It will free up heap space outside of Wasm.

Using all these above strategies, we can surely experience the reduced memory churn, smoother execution, and much less risk of fragmentation or memory leaks, and that too even under stress testing.

Multithreading, Parallelism, and Concurrency

We now look into the high-performance scenarios that demand true parallel computation. We see to the opportunities where we can leverage multicore CPUs for faster data processing, real-time analytics, and smooth user experiences, right inside the browser.

WebAssembly Threads

The WebAssembly threads are enabled by two features:

- **SharedArrayBuffer** in JavaScript, and
- the **threads proposal** for Wasm itself.

When building with Emscripten, we can automatically generate the modules that take advantage of threads, using **`-s USE_PTHREADS=1`** during compilation:

```
emcc matrix.cpp -O3 -s USE_PTHREADS=1 -o matrix_mt.js
```

This result bundles both the Wasm module and support JS code to spin up threads behind the scenes using Web Workers.

Shared Memory and Atomic Operations

The Wasm exposes a global linear memory buffer flagged as **`shared`** to safely share data between the threads. All these threads (main and workers) read and write to shared memory, and atomic operations (**`i32.atomic.rmw.add`**, etc.) to ensure updates happen without race conditions.

Following is a quick sample program:

```
#include <atomic>
extern "C" {
  void atomic_increment(int* counter) {
    std::atomic<int>* p =
reinterpret_cast<std::atomic<int>*>(counter);
    p->fetch_add(1, std::memory_order_relaxed);
  }
```

```
}
```

In practice, we use mutexes, spinlocks, and atomic primitives for coordination, similar to native threads.

Spawning and Managing Threads

Wirthin our Emscripten JS glue, we can easily call the **`PThread_create`** or make use of the **`Module.pthread`** APIs to launch new threads:

```
var thread = Module._pthread_create(0, 0,
Module._worker_function, argPtr);
```

the worker threads execute Wasm routines in parallel. It shares the work (for example, dividing a large image into chunks for simultaneous filtering). We can monitor the thread creation, completion, and resource cleanup using the Wasm hooks.

Parallel Algorithms in Wasm

There are some ommon parallel patterns that include:

- **Divide and Conquer** in which large datasets (matrices, images, simulation grids) are split, each thread operates on a segment.
- **MapReduce and Batch Processing** wherein multiple threads compute results, merge in main thread. And,
- **Producer-Consumer** in which the threads push work into a shared queue, workers consume and process independently.

Any routine that's CPU-bound and can cleanly partition data is a candidate for parallelization.

For example, consider **`matrix_multiply_mt`** which is a function that divides work among threads, and each updating a portion of the output buffer. The main thread initializes workers, distributes pointers/offsets, and merges results, all using shared Wasm memory. This pattern scales computation with available CPU cores for immense speedups in real-world data applications.

Lazy Loading, Code Splitting, and Deferred Execution

There are times when it just isn't efficient to load the whole module at the start. These days, people expect apps to start instantly and only download or initialise heavier features when needed. That's where things like lazy loading, code splitting and deferred execution come in. We'll take a look at how we set up these approaches to boost performance.

Lazy Loading Modules

Lazy loading means we only fetch, compile, and instantiate our Wasm code at the moment it's actually required. For example, if our matrix multiplication feature is only triggered when the user clicks a button, we keep the default UI lean, and postpone Wasm loading:

```
document.getElementById('actionBtn').onclick = async () => {
  if (!window.matrixModule) {
    const response = await fetch('matrix.wasm');
    const bytes = await response.arrayBuffer();
    const instance = await WebAssembly.instantiate(bytes);
    window.matrixModule = instance;
  }
  // Now, use the loaded instance:
  window.matrixModule.exports.matrix_multiply();
};
```

In the above, it reduces the initial load time and improves the perceived responsiveness.

Code Splitting

Very often, the large Wasm projects can be divided into logical sections such as the matrix operations, image filters, signal processing. With **code splitting**, we can bundle each feature's Wasm code separately and load only what the user actually needs. Emscripten and other bundlers allow outputting multiple **.wasm** files.

For example, let us consider that we have **matrix.wasm** and **filter.wasm**. Now here, when the user switches to a new tab or mode in the app, we can fetch and initialize only the necessary file as shown below:

```
async function loadModule(feature) {
  const response = await fetch(feature + '.wasm');
  const bytes = await response.arrayBuffer();
  return await WebAssembly.instantiate(bytes);
}
```

Deferred Execution and Staged Loading

And for really big modules, we might even stage the work, loading the minimum boot logic first and then streaming in advanced features as background activity. If your browser supports Wasm streaming compilation, it can start using Wasm as it's downloading, which reduces wait times even more:

```
const response = fetch('huge_module.wasm');

// Use instantiateStreaming for supported browsers:

const instance = await
WebAssembly.instantiateStreaming(response);
```

This method keeps the UI interactive while heavier code is still coming in.

By combining lazy loading, code splitting, and deferred execution, we significantly reduce startup times, cut unnecessary downloads, and create a smoother, more scalable user experience for all Wasm-based projects.

Caching and Efficient Deployment Strategies

One of the most important things for making Wasm applications fast, reliable and scalable is efficient caching and deployment. Now, let's take a look at the subtopics we need to focus on service worker, browser caching, CDN and HTTP/2 deployment, server-side caching, and version management.

Service Worker and Browser Caching

The service workers let Wasm and JS assets be cached right in the browser, so users get really fast load times when they visit a site again. Let's take a look at how the caching layer actually works in practice:

To start with, we need to register a service worker in our main HTML page:

```
if ('serviceWorker' in navigator) {

  navigator.serviceWorker.register('/sw.js');

}
```

In **`/sw.js`**, we then intercept the **`.wasm`** requests. If the module is in local cache, we then serve it immediately otherwise, we then fetch, store, and respond accordingly:

```
self.addEventListener('fetch', event => {

  if (event.request.url.endsWith('.wasm')) {

    event.respondWith(
```

```
        caches.open('wasm-modules').then(cache =>
          cache.match(event.request).then(response => {
            if (response) return response;
            return fetch(event.request).then(networkRes => {
              cache.put(event.request, networkRes.clone());
              return networkRes;
            });
          })
        )
      );
    }
});
```

This pattern works for updates as well, by changing URLs or cache keys, new versions are picked up on the next load.

HTTP/2 and CDN Optimization

For true global scale, we must combine browser cache with best-in-class server-side delivery. The CDNs distribute **`.wasm`** files worldwide, putting assets close to users geographically. We can use the HTTP/2 features like multiplexing (multiple assets fetched in parallel, no blocking), aggressive caching headers, and pre-compressed files to maximize speed. WebAssembly binaries should ideally be compressed with Brotli for best results:

```
Cache-Control: public, max-age=31536000
Content-Encoding: br
```

When it's time to deploy, each .wasm and JS asset gets a unique filename (module.20251016.wasm), which makes sure that the cache is invalidated straight away if there's an upgrade. The CDNs can be configured to cache for months or years, but can be updated in the background using cache-purge APIs.

When new versions roll out, update the asset manifest and invalidate only the changed assets, not the whole app bundle. If a server or CDN error occurs, service workers can fallback to last-known-good versions.

Server-Side Caching and Cloud Functions

On the serverless platforms like the Cloudflare Workers or the AWS Lambda@Edge, or the Node microservices, the Wasm modules are often loaded repeatedly during heavy traffic.

So here, if we maintain a hot pool of Wasm instances, the server-side code can avoid cold starts, and thereby it can keep the frequently used modules in memory.

Here's what you need to do:

- You can pre-heat a set of Wasm modules when you launch the app.
- Just make sure you store the loaded modules in a Redis/Memcached or simple in-memory store.
- Just a heads-up that we should rotate out idle/expired modules and replenish the pool proactively.

This dramatically reduces latency for APIs or microservices serving Wasm workloads to thousands of users in parallel.

This system is really efficient. It loads super quickly and the upgrades are a breeze. If we give each delivery subtopic the care it needs and combine them into the devops workflow, we can make Wasm apps scalable and resilient for any user, anywhere in the world.

Summary

Throughout this chapter, we experienced the performance engineering lifecycle for WebAssembly modules. Both measurement and optimization areas were well explored. The practical profiling was well demonstrated using browser tools, performance APIs, and flame graphs, leading to hands-on benchmarking techniques for real programs like matrix multiplication. We learned to minimize allocations, tune linear memory, and avoid fragmentation in order to sustain consistent runtime efficiency.

Later, we then learned the advanced concurrency patterns, in which we leaveraged the multithreading through SharedArrayBuffer and atomic operations for scalable parallelism. Lazy loading and code splitting strategies were implemented to improve initial load times and user experience by deferring heavy features. Finally, we examined robust caching and deployment practices, giving equal attention to service workers, CDN edge delivery, server-side pooling, and versioned upgrades. Each step was supported by example code and practical workflow advice, ensuring that high-performance Wasm delivery is achievable and sustainable for any real-world deployment.

CHAPTER 7: PRACTICAL MIGRATION TO WASM 2.0

In this chapter, we are going to step through a real, hands-on journey of migrating a WebAssembly 1.0 project to Wasm 2.0. Up until now, our projects and pipelines have all been set up with the features, conventions, and limitations of Wasm 1.0 in mind. But moving to Wasm 2.0 is not just a small update. It is a meaningful jump that brings new reliability, better performance, and long-term options for scaling web and cloud software. And, to really succeed with this migration, we need to do more than just update a version number or patch a few build scripts. So here, we will take stock of every module, every bit of glue logic, every build tool, and all supporting documents that make up our current Wasm project. Once this is mapped, we'll spot what needs to change and design a practical, low-risk upgrade plan.

In the next topic, we will break this process down and see exactly how to begin.

Project Assessment and Migration Planning

Auditing Codebase

We always start with a full mapping of our Wasm project. So, first, we will make a list of all Wasm modules, any JavaScript glue code, and every library or tool that is tied into our build and deployment pipelines. For instance, let us say our main module is **`dist/image.wasm`**, which has been built from **`src/wasmimage.cpp`** using the Emscripten toolchain. And, in the browser, we are loading this using **`src/js/loader.js`**, which carries some custom memory handling and function exports. We will also note any third-party libraries, like **`libpng`** or **`libjpeg`**, because these often need separate migration steps.

At this point, we should open up a document or spreadsheet and start jotting down:

- Every Wasm artifact and where it comes from
- The scripts or tools (like Makefiles or CI configs) that build or link these artifacts
- Every library with its version
- A quick note if anything looks dependent on deprecated features, memory techniques, or Emscripten-specific APIs that might not work right in Wasm 2.0

Once we have this inventory, the migration already feels less overwhelming.

Identifying Migration Points and Dependencies

Now, we look closer at how all these parts are glued together. For example,

- Does the glue code make heavy use of **`Module.malloc`**, **`Module.free`**, or direct buffer manipulations?
- Are there pieces that plug into browser APIs, or is there server-side logic that expects the older Wasm 1.0 binary layout?

When we are doing it, we also need to keep an eye out for any Emscripten-specific patterns or custom metadata sections that might not fit neatly into the Wasm 2.0 workflow. Also, it is important to check the third-party libraries we use. Some older libraries, especially those only ever compiled against Wasm 1.0, might not yet be compatible with new features like native SIMD or exception handling. It'd be good to make a note of each one, so we can either find versions that fully support Wasm 2.0 or be ready to rebuild them with updated toolchains.

Test Coverage Planning and Staged Rollout

So before we get started, let's have a look at the tests. The idea is to know exactly what 'correct' looks like. So, let's make sure we've got good coverage for all our Wasm interfaces and features – unit, integration and end-to-end. At this point, it's a good idea to write new or extended tests that specifically check Wasm 2.0 behaviour and tricky migration edge cases. If we can, we'll add feature flags or environment toggles so we can test the new Wasm 2.0 modules in staging environments, with minimum risk to production.

The best way to stay on top of things is to have a migration checklist as shown below:

- Backup or snapshot the full project before any upgrades
- Update build tool and library versions
- Check dependency compatibility
- Roll out deployments in controlled steps
- Outline a rollback plan in case something does not work as expected

If we work through the above steps with focus and transparency, we can stop our Wasm 2.0 migration from being a risky 'big-bang' rewrite and instead become a careful, well-orchestrated upgrade.

Refactoring Legacy Interfaces for Wasm 2.0

Now that we've finished planning and auditing our project, the next important step is to tackle the actual interfaces that tie our Wasm modules to the rest of the codebase. A lot of production projects built on Wasm 1.0 are closely linked to old patterns, especially the connections between WebAssembly, JavaScript glue code, and the environments they're running in. If we want Wasm 2.0 to work smoothly and make use of its new features, we need to spend some time reworking these connections.

To kick things off, we're going to take a look at the common legacy interface issues that'll need to be dealt with during migration.

Updating Function Imports, Exports, and Glue Logic

Most of the Wasm 1.0 projects define module imports and exports using the patterns offered by Emscripten. For example, we might have glue code that relies on the classic **`Module`** object in JavaScript, is littered with calls to **`Module._functionName`**, or handles memory via raw heap pointers and offset math.

So, to move toward Wasm 2.0, we need to replace or upgrade this pattern. So, let us say that our Wasm module exports two main functions, **add** and **multiply**, and our previous glue code looks like this:

```
// Old Way, Wasm 1.0 with Emscripten-generated Module object
const resultAdd = Module._add(5, 3);
const resultMultiply = Module._multiply(2, 8);
```

In Wasm 2.0, we want a more direct and standard approach. Once we are done with compiling our module to the Wasm 2.0 binary, we then import it into JavaScript using the standard WebAssembly API. For this, we first fetch and instantiate the binary, then load and invoke the exported functions as in the below sample code:

```
// New Way, Wasm 2.0 standard API
const response = await fetch('dist/image.wasm');
const bytes = await response.arrayBuffer();
const { instance } = await WebAssembly.instantiate(bytes);
const resultAdd = instance.exports.add(5, 3);
const resultMultiply = instance.exports.multiply(2, 8);
```

In the above, we shift from custom **Module** logic to native **WebAssembly.instantiate**. This simplifies the maintenance and make our interfaces more readable. This upgrade process can involve changing dozens of call sites, so it is best to track them in the migration spreadsheet and update in clear, small commits.

Refactoring Memory Access and Management

In many legacy Wasm projects, the memory management is handled manually, possibly with direct access to **Module.HEAPU8**, pointer math, and custom allocation routines. The Wasm 2.0, however, introduces safer ways to request and manage memory, making it easier to avoid buffer overflows and inconsistencies.

In the following, we will see the behavior of a typical memory access pattern in Wasm 1.0:

```
// Old Way, direct memory access with Emscripten
const ptr = Module._malloc(1024);
const buffer = new Uint8Array(Module.HEAPU8.buffer, ptr,
1024);
// Use the buffer...
```

```
Module._free(ptr);
```

Now, to modernize this for Wasm 2.0, we need to move to managed memory exports or typed accessor functions as shown below:

```
// New Way, memory exported by Wasm 2.0 module
const memory = instance.exports.memory;
const buffer = new Uint8Array(memory.buffer, offset, length);
// Access and manipulate buffer as needed
```

To sum up, we reference the exported **`memory`** and handle buffers through standard APIs, reducing hidden bugs and aligning with future Wasm improvements.

Rewriting Host Bindings and Custom Metadata

The next critical step is to revisit our host bindings and any custom metadata that connects our module to outside systems. In Wasm 1.0 projects, it's common to find all sorts of custom logic for analytics, debugging, monitoring, or even inter-module communication. These often rely on homegrown tricks or private hooks which hasworked fine in Wasm 1.0, but aren't guaranteed to play nicely with the evolving standards and features in Wasm 2.0.

Let's walk through how we can take these legacy host bindings and metadata strategies and bring them up to date.

Migrating to Standardized Host Bindings

In Wasm 2.0, there are several features that help us move away from brittle custom glue. Let us consider that earlier we injected analytics markers as below:

```
# Non-standard: patching binary after build
python inject_metadata.py dist/image.wasm --key=analytics_v1 -
-value="enabled"
```

Now, we can use standard tools or build flags provided by Wasm-aware compilers and bundlers to add custom sections in a way that is fully supported as shown below:

```
# Modern way with wasm-tools
wasm-tools add-custom-section dist/image.wasm analytics_v1
enabled
```

And, from JavaScript or another host language, we can retrieve this metadata using up-to-date APIs rather than manual parsing.

Refactoring Communication Channels

Another example comes from logging and debugging. In Wasm 1.0, we might've routed logs back to JS with a custom import like this:

```
// Legacy JS glue
const imports = {
  env: {
    log: ptr => {
      const message = decodeString(ptr); // manual
      sendToAnalytics(message);
    }
  }
};
```

When Wasm 2.0 comes along, and especially when runtimes adopt the interface types proposal, we can define these expected bindings declaratively. We're not just talking about the existence of logs, but also the type, shape, and any restrictions on what data gets passed. This means less chance of things going wrong as the Wasm ecosystem develops.

If we go through these refactoring steps methodically, the project will become compatible with Wasm 2.0, and we'll also lay the foundation for faster maintenance, more reliable deployments and easier upgrades in the future.

Adapting Build Tools and Conversion Scripts

Now that we have handled the necessary interface and metadata refactoring, our next important step is to update our build tools and automation pipelines for Wasm 2.0. This part of the migration is absolutely crucial because an outdated, misconfigured, or incompatible build process can lead to subtle bugs, missing features, or even complete deployment failures.

So, let us walk through the exact steps and choices we make as we bring our build systems up-to-date for WebAssembly 2.0.

Auditing and Upgrading Toolchain

The very first thing we do is to pin down which tools we are using for compiling, linking, bundling, and testing. For most real Wasm projects, this typically involves a mix of:

- C/C++ compilers

- Emscripten or WASI SDK as the main toolchains
- JavaScript/TypeScript bundlers for web workflows
- Python, Shell, Make, or Bash for automation

We want to check the versions of each tool in our stack. For Wasm 2.0, toolchain authors often release new features incrementally, so even a minor version can make a difference. Let us start by looking for:

- Minimum supported versions for Wasm 2.0 features (SIMD, extended exports, new section formats)
- Official Wasm 2.0 support notes or migration tips in the release notes or documentation
- Community feedback and issues from projects that already migrated

Once we confirm that all tools in our workflow support Wasm 2.0, we record the specific version changes and note any flags or configs that need adjustment.

Updating Build Scripts and CI Pipelines

Next, we then get on to update our build automation. Let's suppose we have a **`Makefile`**, a **`build.sh`**, or YAML files for GitHub Actions, Jenkins, or GitLab CI. Here, we will:

1. Replace old tool invocations with new ones that explicitly target Wasm 2.0.
2. Add any new compiler flags or options required. For example, Emscripten and Clang might add a **`-wasm2`** or **`--enable-wasm2`** flag to opt-in to version 2.0 features.
3. Add pre- and post-build steps to validate the module. For instance, we might integrate tools like **`wasm-tools validate`** or browser-based test runners.

Given below is how a simple script update could look like:

```
# Old command

emcc src/wasmimage.cpp -o dist/image.wasm

# New command for Wasm 2.0, adding flag and integrating
validation

emcc src/wasmimage.cpp -o dist/image.wasm --enable-wasm2

wasm-tools validate dist/image.wasm
```

If we use continuous integration, make sure to update the runner's build environments, so every build gets the correct tooling by default.

Automating Deployment Checks and Feature Gates

A good migration always includes a way to test and limit new features in production. Here, we add feature gates or environment variables within our scripts and deployment manifests so we can flip Wasm 2.0 support on or off easily.

For example, in Node.js or the browser, we might expose a toggle like this:

```
const wasmFile = process.env.ENABLE_WASM2
  ? 'dist/image-wasm2.wasm'
  : 'dist/image.wasm';
```

And, in CI or shell automation, we'll run both builds until we are confident in the migration's stability.

Integrating wasm-tools for Continuous Validation

Let us take a concrete example. We want every new build to get checked for Wasm 2.0 specification compliance before it lands in production. So, inside our CI, we can automate this step:

```
# GitHub Actions example (snippet)
steps:
  - name: Build Wasm module (Wasm 2.0)
    run: emcc src/main.cpp -o dist/app.wasm --enable-wasm2
  - name: Validate Wasm module
    run: wasm-tools validate dist/app.wasm
```

Every build will now fail if the output is not fully Wasm 2.0-compliant, making problems visible early.

By the end of this toolchain adaptation and automation phase, the entire pipeline, right from first compile to final deployment, will be Wasm 2.0 aware, tested, and easy for every contributor to understand.

Module Linking, Component Model, and Inter-Module Migration

Our next focus is going to be upgrading the overall architecture of our Wasm modules and components. The Wasm 2.0 introduces several changes in how modules link together, how imports and exports work, and even how custom sections and dependencies are handled. So, here, we will make sure that both the core modules and their integration points of our project are ready for future scaling, easier updates, and proper separation of concerns.

In the following, we will unpack what this transition looks like in a production-ready codebase.

Analyzing Module Structure and Interdependencies

First, we take a close look at how our application is split into modules. Many legacy Wasm 1.0 projects bundle everything into a single monolithic binary, which can make upgrades and debugging tricky. In Wasm 2.0, we have new ways of linking modules together, expressing dependencies, and organizing code for more efficient builds and maintenance.

We start by listing out all modules, including the core logic, helper utilities, feature-specific components, and platform adapters. For each, we check:

- Which modules consume or produce shared resources (memory, exports, tables)
- Which rely on direct imports/exports vs. custom integration hacks
- Which are reusable and which are tightly bound to project-specific logic

This analysis tells us where big refactoring efforts will pay off.

Refactoring for Module Linking and Separation

The Wasm 2.0 brings the module linking proposal, allowing modules to reference each other using standard section formats and host-managed glue code. So, what we're going to do now is separate our concerns: take tightly coupled features, split them into distinct modules, and link them using Wasm 2.0's native mechanisms.

For example, let us assume that our project has a math module, an image processsor, and a UI adapter. So here, instead of compiling these into one binary, we can do the following:

```
# Build each module independently
emcc src/math.cpp -o dist/math.wasm --enable-wasm2
emcc src/image.cpp -o dist/image.wasm --enable-wasm2
# Then link or load them as components in the JS runtime
```

Here, in the above script, we load these modules separately and establish links between them, leveraging official APIs and avoiding brittle hacks. In the browser, it might look like:

```
// Load modules and connect via imports
const mathModule = await loadWasm('dist/math.wasm');
const imageModule = await loadWasm('dist/image.wasm', {
  imports: { math: mathModule.exports }
```

```
});
```

Because of how it's designed, upgrades are a breeze. If we want to improve the math kernel, for example, we can just rebuild and deploy that module without having to touch the whole app.

Cross-Version Compatibility and Hybrid Serving

Once the module migration is done, we need to make sure we've got solid safeguards in place for compatibility and quality. When we move to Wasm 2.0, it's not a one-size-fits-all situation. We still have to support older environments, and we're keen to catch any unexpected bugs that might pop up during the transition. Now, I'll explain how we can make cross-version compatibility a reality and make regression testing a regular part of the workflow.

Designing Dual Compatibility

First, we recognize that not all client browsers, backend runtimes, or third-party modules will support Wasm 2.0 right away. So, as we roll out the migration, we continue to build and ship Wasm 1.0 binaries alongside their Wasm 2.0 replacements.

In the following, we will see how it works in a deployment scenario:

- Within the build process, we create both **module-wasm1.wasm** and **module-wasm2.wasm**.
- Then we write the glue logic, either in JavaScript, Rust, or Python to detect Wasm 2.0 support at runtime:

```
function getWasmBinary() {
  if (supportsWasm2()) {
    return 'dist/module-wasm2.wasm';
  }
  return 'dist/module-wasm1.wasm';
}
function supportsWasm2() {
  // Use feature detection or user agent checks here
  // Replace with robust detection if using advanced features
  return typeof WebAssembly.validate === 'function';
}
```

```
const binaryFile = getWasmBinary();
// Load and instantiate the chosen binary as usual
```

By offering both binaries, every platform can load the version it can handle, seamlessly.

Role of Adapters and Polyfills

The exported API shapes can sometimes differ between Wasm 1.0 and Wasm 2.0 when working with external libraries or legacy modules. When that happens, we just write a simple adapter or polyfill. For example, if Wasm 2.0 brings in new import types or custom sections, we wrap those features in safe runtime checks, and switch to the old methods when needed.

To give you an idea: If Wasm 2.0 exports enhanced error reporting via new custom sections, we check for them before using them:t

```
if ('error_metadata' in instance.exports) {
  // Use Wasm 2.0 error features
} else {
  // Fall back to legacy error handling
}
```

Building Robust Regression Test Suites

No migration is complete without thorough, repeatable tests. At this stage, our goal is to make sure Wasm 2.0 doesn't break anything that worked in Wasm 1.0 and that new features behave as expected.

Given below is how we approach this:

- Before migration, we run the full suite of unit, integration, and live tests against the Wasm 1.0 build to establish baseline "correct" behavior.
- We then build Wasm 2.0 versions, then run all the same tests, comparing outputs, performance, and error logs side-by-side.
- After this, we then add new test cases for Wasm 2.0-only features, edge cases, and buffer sizes.
- We make use of automated CI systems to ensure every commit, merge, or deploy runs full regression checks for both versions.
- Incase on failure, we then log errors, rollback the release, and record fixes in the migration documentation.

If we keep a matrix of test results for both Wasm versions, we can spot subtle bugs and check that our compatibility logic works in the field. If we make sure the migration process is based on systematic compatibility handling and robust regression testing, we can make Wasm 2.0 easy for developers and users to adopt, and safe and manageable too.

Migration Documentation and Knowledge Base

Next time we move the project to Wasm 2.0, a good set of docs doesn't have to mean loads of paperwork. Instead, it's more about taking notes that help everyone on the team and even future you understand what changed, why it changed and how to fix things quickly if something breaks.

I'll explain how we can do this without creating extra work or getting lost in "corporate" writing:

Keep Change Log

Whenever we make a migration change (switch a module, update a build script, change an API), jot it down in a simple file called **`MIGRATION.md`** (or use the project's README).

Also, we must note the date, what we changed, and why it was changed.

We can see the following example:

```
2025-10-17: Updated build script for Wasm 2.0. Switched from emcc to wasm-tools. Needed for new section format.

2025-10-18: Rewrote image processing module to use SIMD. Faster performance, but only works on Wasm 2.0 browsers.
```

List Problems and Fixing Them

So here, if we hit an error or something does not work while migrating, write down what happened and the solution. And, if we had to rollback, note exactly what we did to undo the change.

Following is a good example to understand:

```
Problem: "Build failed with wasm-tools validate"

Fix: Upgraded wasm-tools to latest version, added --enable-wasm2 flag.

Rollback: Restored old dist/module-wasm1.wasm for compatibility.
```

Simple How-To Guides

Here, we simply just sketch out some basic instructions for new team members (or for ourself, in six months' time) on how to build, test and roll back Wasm 2.0 features.

Following is a simple example to just give you an idea:

```
To build: run 'emcc src/main.cpp -o dist/app.wasm --enable-wasm2'

To test: run 'wasm-tools validate dist/app.wasm'

If Wasm 2.0 breaks: remove 'dist/app.wasm', replace with 'dist/app-wasm1.wasm'
```

Add List of Tools

Somewhere in the doc, we need to note which tool versions we used, so we can set up new environments or fix issues in the future.

Following is an example:

```
Tool Versions:

- Emscripten 3.1.10

- wasm-tools 1.2.3
```

That's really all we need for migration documentation. The idea is to help you, the team, and future maintainers get things working quickly.

Summary

To sum up the understanding, we gained a practical understanding to migrate a WebAssembly 1.0 project to Wasm 2.0. We learned to audit the existing modules, dependencies, and glue code, and created a detailed map of each impacted artifact by the migration. We recognized the importance of planning, keeping all changes documented, and identifying the core features that needed careful attention when upgrading to Wasm 2.0.

We learned to update build tools and automation pipelines for Wasm 2.0 compliance, while also supporting dual operation for compatibility with Wasm 1.0 users. We witnessed practically to handle the feature migration safely by using fallbacks and regression testing, and we adopted solid module linking strategies to allow for future project scaling and modularization. Finally, all migration phases were carefully recorded in a simple, accessible log, and the knowledge gained was organized in a way that helps both current and future contributors troubleshoot and enhance the project with confidence.

Chapter 8: Using WebAssembly with Dapr

In the previous chapter, we learned to modernize the modules and workflows, and also built a strong foundation for maintainability and future growth. With the upgraded Wasm project in place, it is time to take the next step, wherein we learn to integrate WebAssembly with advanced platform tools that streamline microservices and event-driven architectures. In this chapter, we will see how connecting the Wasm modules to Dapr opens up the powerful patterns for service invocation, state management, pub/sub messaging, and secure communication between services, both in the cloud and at the edge. We will discover how Dapr's sidecar architecture enables we to run, scale, and observe Wasm-powered workloads as part of robust distributed systems, without having to handcraft all the underlying plumbing.

By the end of this chapter, we will understand the newly migrated Wasm projects, and the way it participate in cutting-edge cloud architectures, gain access to Dapr's powerful building blocks, and set the stage for innovation at any scale.

Dapr and WebAssembly Integration

When we finish migrating the Wasm modules, the immediate challenge becomes integrating them into modern, cloud-native architectures, especially if we want the application to scale, communicate across different languages, and manage distributed data and events reliably. Traditionally, connecting all these dots has meant writing a ton of custom code: setting up HTTP clients, wiring up message brokers, handling retries, encrypting traffic, and managing state. But as projects grow, maintaining this plumbing gets time-consuming and fragile.

This is exactly where Dapr steps in and changes the game. Dapr is an open-source runtime designed to simplify building and operating microservices on any platform. Instead of scattering infrastructure logic across every codebase, Dapr provides a set of common building blocks like service invocation, state management, pub/sub messaging, secrets management, and observability as simple APIs. The best part is that these APIs work seamlessly across Go, Python, JavaScript, Java, Rust, and even WebAssembly.

Dapr Sidecar Model

Now we will understand how it really works. Let us think that we have a Wasm module that processes images, a Go service that handles user authentication, and a Python service that sends notifications. With the power of Dapr, each of the service runs its own lightweight "sidecar" process, which listens on a local port and exposes Dapr's APIs. When our Wasm module finishes processing, it doesn't need to know how to talk to Redis or Kafka or a remote HTTP server, instead, it simply calls a local endpoint like:

`http://localhost:3500/v1.0/state/store`

or publishes an event to:

`http://localhost:3500/v1.0/publish/pubsub`

The Dapr sidecar handles the real complexity of discovering other services, retrying failed requests, encrypting communication, and persisting state. This sidecar pattern means we can develop, test, and run each microservice independently, all while leveraging the power of the broader Dapr service mesh.

Dapr's Building Blocks

We will now look at the break down of the main Dapr building blocks and how they improve the entire WebAssembly integration:

Service Invocation

The Wasm module can call functions in another service (whether that's Node.js, Rust, or Go) just by hitting a Dapr endpoint. We don't need to know physical server addresses or handle HTTP retries theself. For example, after transforming data, the Wasm module can trigger a remote notification service simply by a standard HTTP call. Dapr does the lookup and delivery.

State Management

Need to store or retrieve state from inside the Wasm code? Instead of hardcoding Redis, CosmosDB, or PostgreSQL clients, we use Dapr's state API. The backend can be swapped at any time without changing the interface in the module.

Pub/Sub Messaging

If the Wasm module wants to broadcast a message when a task is complete, then we send the event via Dapr's pub/sub API. The Dapr ensures delivery and manages all the broker details behind the scenes.

Secrets Management

Suppose the Wasm logic needs to access API keys or credentials, but we don't want to bake them into the code or environment variables. Dapr offers a standard API for secrets, supporting secure vaults like HashiCorp Vault or Azure Key Vault.

Observability

When issues crop up, the tracing and logging allows us to see every message and state transition from the module, across the whole microservice mesh, even if you're working with Wasm code that would otherwise be tough to debug in a distributed setup.

Why Dapr?

The Wasm gives performance, portability, and security to the computational tasks. But as soon as we need those Wasm modules to talk to a database, publish events, or interact with external services, the Dapr lifts away the heavy lifting from the code, offering ready-made APIs and operational features. This means the Wasm modules become truly language- and platform-agnostic components in the cloud or edge systems.

For example, we might deploy an image-processing plugin as a Wasm module. With Dapr, this plugin can store results, publish notifications, and even authenticate with other services, all using standard Dapr APIs. We never have to rewrite code just because we want to change the underlying infrastructure, move to another cloud, or include a new runtime.

If you're coming from a monolithic or hand-wired system, Dapr may seem like a big leap. But once we see how it handles networking, error handling, observability, and service location for you, we will realize we can focus on business logic instead of "yak shaving." The code gets leaner, easier to test, and much more resilient.

In the next topics, we will walk through concrete setup, configure the sidecars, map out the APIs we want to use, and decide which Dapr components fit the use case.

Setting up Dapr

Our next step is to set up a reliable development environment where both Dapr and the Wasm modules can work smoothly together. The setup process ensures the project is ready to take full advantage of Dapr's building blocks and lets us focus on developing Wasm-powered services without worrying about infrastructure details.

Installing Dapr

This is simple to install. We simply open the terminal and run the following:

```
# Download and install the Dapr CLI
wget -q
https://raw.githubusercontent.com/dapr/cli/master/install/inst
all.sh -O - | /bin/bash
# Initialize Dapr runtime (launches necessary containers)
dapr init
```

After initialization, the Dapr runs a set of background services (like Redis for state management) and starts the control plane. We can also check the installation using:

```
dapr --version
```

Preparing Wasm Project Directory

Once Dapr is installed and running, we will want to set up the working directory for a Wasm module project. After this, we then organize the folder with subdirectories for source code, build outputs, configuration files, and scripts.

Following is a sample project directory:

```
my-wasm-dapr-service/
├── src/
│   └── main.c (or .cpp, .rs, etc.)
├── dist/
│   └── module.wasm
├── config/
│   └── components.yaml
├── scripts/
└── README.md
```

The **config/components.yaml** file will later hold the Dapr component definitions (such as state stores, pub/sub brokers, or secret stores).

Configuring Dapr Sidecar

Each time we run the app, we launch it with a Dapr sidecar. To do basic local testing, we can start the Wasm application and the Dapr sidecar using the Dapr CLI:

```
# Run the application's executable with Dapr sidecar
# Replace 'wasm-app' with the WebAssembly runner or service logic command
dapr run --app-id wasm-app --app-port 8080 -- wasm-app
```

Here, the **wasm-app** can be any server or runner that loads and executes the Wasm module. The Dapr sidecar exposes its own API at ports 3500 (HTTP) and 50001 (gRPC) by default, allowing the service logic to call Dapr's features locally without extra network wiring.

Connecting to Dapr APIs

After launching everything, the Wasm code can easily interact with Dapr. And it is done simply by making HTTP calls to the sidecar's endpoints. For example, if the module has logic to store user scores, we can POST JSON data to Dapr's state API at:

http://localhost:3500/v1.0/state/statestore

If we use a language binding or a custom loader for WebAssembly, ensure it can create HTTP requests to these endpoints. Otherwise, set up a simple HTTP proxy or handler in the application runtime to bridge Wasm calls with Dapr APIs.

Next, we'll focus on how to package the WebAssembly modules for Dapr and ensure seamless invocation from other microservices.

Packaging Wasm Modules for Dapr

Now that we've got the Dapr environment and Wasm development directory all set up, we can crack on with packaging the WebAssembly modules so they can be used as Dapr services.

Compiling Wasm Module

So, let's start by building a simple Wasm module that can add two numbers, just to get things started. In this example, we'll use C, but the same workflow can be used with Rust or AssemblyScript if you use a supported compiler.

Suppose the source file is named **main.c** in the **src/** directory:

```
// src/main.c
int add(int a, int b) {
    return a + b;
}
```

To compile this to Wasm, use a tool like Emscripten:

```
emcc src/main.c -o dist/module.wasm -s STANDALONE_WASM=1 -s
EXPORTED_FUNCTIONS='["_add"]'
```

Now the **dist/module.wasm** contains the compiled module, ready for use.

Running Wasm Host Process

The WebAssembly modules generally need a host process to load and execute them. We can use a Wasm runtime, such as Wasmtime, Wasmer, or WasmEdge, as the main process. This process will act as the HTTP (or gRPC) server Dapr expects for service invocation. For this example, let's use Wasmtime and a small Node.js wrapper to handle HTTP requests and invoke Wasm functions.

The first thing we do is setting up a basic Node.js HTTP server to load the Wasm module:

```
// scripts/wasm-server.js
```

```
const http = require('http');
const fs = require('fs');
const { WASI } = require('wasi');
const wasi = new WASI();
const wasmBuffer = fs.readFileSync('./dist/module.wasm');
WebAssembly.instantiate(wasmBuffer, { wasi_snapshot_preview1:
wasi.wasiImport })
  .then(obj => {
    const add = obj.instance.exports.add;
    http.createServer((req, res) => {
      if (req.url === '/add' && req.method === 'POST') {
        let body = '';
        req.on('data', chunk => { body += chunk; });
        req.on('end', () => {
          const { a, b } = JSON.parse(body);
          const result = add(a, b);
          res.writeHead(200, { 'Content-Type':
'application/json' });
          res.end(JSON.stringify({ result }));
        });
      } else {
        res.writeHead(404);
        res.end();
      }
    }).listen(8080, () => {
      console.log('Wasm server running on port 8080');
    });
  });
```

From the above, the small server listens for POST requests to **/add**, parses incoming JSON `{ "a": 5, "b": 3 }`, calls the Wasm **add** function, and responds with `{ "result": 8 }`.

Registering Service to Dapr

After this, we then launch the server with Dapr:

```
dapr run --app-id wasm-add --app-port 8080 -- node
scripts/wasm-server.js
```

From this, the Dapr exposes the Wasm-powered service to the rest of the ecosystem. Any other Dapr service, no matter its language, can now call the app through Dapr's service invocation API:

```
curl -X POST http://localhost:3500/v1.0/invoke/wasm-
add/method/add -H "Content-Type: application/json" -d
'{"a":2,"b":4}'
```

This sends the request to Dapr, which forwards it to the Wasm server's **/add** endpoint.

To sum up, the service is now discoverable and callable by any other Dapr service, fully unlocking the power of language-agnostic, plug-in business logic in a cloud-native application. We can expand the pattern for more Wasm functions or different runtimes as the needs grow.

Calling Wasm from Other Dapr Services

Now that we have packaged the Wasm module as a service exposed through Dapr, we now look into how to put it into action. In the following, we will see how we can call the Wasm service from both Go and Python Dapr apps and make use of Wasm as a reusable business logic engine.

Calling Wasm Module from Go Dapr

Now that we have the Dapr-enabled Wasm service running, as shown earlier but let us assume that, we want to create a Go service that invokes the Wasm module using Dapr's HTTP API for service invocation. So here, we start by initializing a simple Go web server. This service will accept requests, forward them to the Wasm module using the Dapr HTTP endpoint, and relay the response.

Following is a sample program:

```
// main.go

package main
```

```
import (
    "bytes"
    "encoding/json"
    "io/ioutil"
    "log"
    "net/http"
)
type AddRequest struct {
    A int `json:"a"`
    B int `json:"b"`
}
type AddResponse struct {
    Result int `json:"result"`
}
func main() {
    http.HandleFunc("/sum", func(w http.ResponseWriter, r
*http.Request) {
        var req AddRequest
        json.NewDecoder(r.Body).Decode(&req)
        body, _ := json.Marshal(req)
        resp, err := http.Post(
            "http://localhost:3500/v1.0/invoke/wasm-
add/method/add",
            "application/json", bytes.NewBuffer(body))
        if err != nil {
            w.WriteHeader(http.StatusInternalServerError)
            w.Write([]byte("Dapr call failed"))
            return
        }
        defer resp.Body.Close()
```

```
        resBody, _ := ioutil.ReadAll(resp.Body)
        var daprResp AddResponse
        json.Unmarshal(resBody, &daprResp)
        json.NewEncoder(w).Encode(daprResp)
    })
    log.Println("Go service running on :8081")
    http.ListenAndServe(":8081", nil)
}
```

In the above script, every time we POST to **/sum**, the Go service makes an HTTP POST to the Wasm Dapr service using Dapr's service invocation endpoint, then sends the result back to the client.

After this, we then launch the Go service through Dapr as well, for automatic discovery:

```
dapr run --app-id go-sum --app-port 8081 -- go run main.go
```

Calling Wasm Module from Python Dapr

We again do the same with Python as we learned to call the wasm module from Go Dapr. Now to do this for Python, we will create a small Flask or FastAPI service which acts as a client to the Wasm module.

```
# app.py
import requests
from flask import Flask, request, jsonify
app = Flask(__name__)
@app.route('/sum', methods=['POST'])
def sum_handler():
    data = request.get_json()
    resp = requests.post(
        'http://localhost:3500/v1.0/invoke/wasm-
add/method/add',
        json={'a': data['a'], 'b': data['b']}
    )
```

```
    return jsonify(resp.json())
if __name__ == "__main__":
    app.run(port=8082)
```

After this, we then run the following Python service with Dapr:

```
dapr run --app-id py-sum --app-port 8082 -- python app.py
```

So, any service in the Dapr mesh, whether it's written in Go, Python or any other language, can now call the Wasm business logic using the same Dapr endpoint. All the computational logic (like the add function) runs inside the Wasm module, so it's all consolidated, consistent and language-agnostic.

Writing Business Logic as Decision Engine

We can use Wasm for more than just basic arithmetic as a full business rules engine. So, we want the Wasm module to decide whether to approve or reject a transaction based on simple rules (like an amount limit).

We need to change the C source to implement a decision:

```
// src/decision.c
int approve(int amount) {
    if (amount < 1000) {
        return 1; // approve
    } else {
        return 0; // reject
    }
}
```

We then compile as before:

```
emcc src/decision.c -o dist/decision.wasm -s STANDALONE_WASM=1
-s EXPORTED_FUNCTIONS='["_approve"]'
```

Then, we update the Node.js or runtime server to expose this as a method:

```
// Extend wasm-server.js with an /approve endpoint
http.createServer((req, res) => {
```

```
  // ... (previous logic)
  if (req.url === '/approve' && req.method === 'POST') {
    let body = '';
    req.on('data', chunk => { body += chunk; });
    req.on('end', () => {
      const { amount } = JSON.parse(body);
      const result = approve(amount); // 1 for approve, 0 for
reject
      res.writeHead(200, { 'Content-Type': 'application/json'
});
      res.end(JSON.stringify({ approved: !!result }));
    });
  }
}).listen(8080);
```

From the above, we can say that from any Dapr-connected service (Go, Python, or others), we can call the **approve** business logic through the service invocation endpoint, passing in a transaction amount and receiving a decision. This pattern lets us centralize business rules in Wasm which then allow us to carry out the easy updates, modular deployment, and consistent behavior across the distributed application.

State Management and Pub/Sub

Introduction to Dapr's State Management

We've found that managing application state becomes a central challenge once we start building distributed systems. This state includes anything that needs to be kept between function calls, like user sessions, counters, workflow status, shopping carts, and more. In classic setups, we might hook up Redis, PostgreSQL, or another store on our own, writing custom code for each integration.

But with Dapr, state management is a lot easier and more consistent. It gives you a consistent HTTP (or gRPC) API that lets any service, no matter the language, save, retrieve and delete state objects using just basic API calls. The actual backing store (Redis, Azure CosmosDB, PostgreSQL, etc.) is configured in a Dapr component file, so the app doesn't need to know the details. Fancy switching from Redis to something else? We just tweak Dapr's settings, not the code. This makes adding or changing state management easy and low-risk.

Using Dapr's State Management

We now walk through how the Wasm module can directly interact with Dapr's state API. (Remember, the Wasm module won't make HTTP calls itself; instead, the host process or server that loads the Wasm module will bridge between Wasm code and Dapr's API.)

Let us think of a situation wherein we have a WebAssembly module that needs to save user scores after some computation. So here, at first, the Node.js (or Rust, Go, etc.) runtime exposes an endpoint (e.g., **`/save-score`**) for saving a score. When called, it:

- Receives score info from a client
- Calls into the Wasm module (which might apply business rules, validation, or format the data)
- Uses Node.js HTTP client to forward the state to Dapr's state API

Following is a sample Node.js program:

```
const http = require('http');
const fetch = require('node-fetch');
// Loads and exposes the Wasm function 'processScore'
http.createServer((req, res) => {
  if (req.url === '/save-score' && req.method === 'POST') {
    let body = '';
    req.on('data', chunk => { body += chunk; });
    req.on('end', async () => {
      const { userId, score } = JSON.parse(body);
      // Call into Wasm for any processing
      const processedScore = processScore(score); // from the
Wasm module
      // Now save via Dapr state API
      await
fetch('http://localhost:3500/v1.0/state/statestore', {
        method: 'POST',
        headers: { 'Content-Type': 'application/json' },
        body: JSON.stringify([
          { key: userId, value: processedScore }
```

```
        ])
      });
      res.writeHead(200);
      res.end('Score saved');
    });
  }
}).listen(8080);
```

In the above, the Dapr will automatically persist the key-value state object to the configured backend, such as Redis. Now, to retrieve the score, we had to set up another endpoint, and call the Dapr state GET API.

Using Dapr Pub/Sub

The Dapr's pub/sub capability lets services send and receive messages in an event-driven manner, decoupling the sender from the receiver. The very common use cases are notifications, event broadcasting, and asynchronous workflows.

Following is how we can publish events from a Wasm-powered service:

- The Wasm module produces a result (say, a new order is processed)
- The host runtime (Node.js/Python) exposes an endpoint, e.g., **`/publish-event`**, and bridges any event output from Wasm code to the Dapr pub/sub endpoint

Following is a sample Publish Example:

```
// ... inside the HTTP handler
await fetch('http://localhost:3500/v1.0/publish/pubsub/new-orders', {
  method: 'POST',
  headers: { 'Content-Type': 'application/json' },
  body: JSON.stringify({ orderId, amount: processedAmount })
});
```

In the above sample, if we want to subscribe to these events, any other Dapr-enabled service just registers an endpoint that Dapr will POST to when a new event arrives. The wasmpoweredservice only needs to publish, and the Dapr runtime takes care of routing and delivery.

It's all thanks to Dapr's state and pub/sub APIs, which are used through the host process. This means that WebAssembly modules can store persistent data and participate in real-time, event-driven workflows, all without needing to be directly connected to infrastructure or cloud wiring. The pattern lets the Wasm code contribute fully in modern, cloud-native apps, whether you're keeping user history, reacting to events, or building scalable systems.

Running Wasm Modules in Production

Once we've developed, packaged and integrated the Wasm services within the Dapr ecosystem, the next step is to get these services into production. It's really easy to use WebAssembly with Dapr, whether we are just testing something out or we need to scale it up big time. We can even do it inside Kubernetes clusters or on our favourite cloud provider. Here, we'll focus on showing you how to bring everything together step by step for both local/staging and production-like deployments.

Local and Staging Deployment

Let us start with local environments, where we have already used the **dapr run** command for manual launches during development. For staging or automated testing, we will want to use either docker-compose or Dapr's built-in components, allowing we to bring up the Wasm service, sidecars, and dependencies together.

Following is the sample Docker Compose setup:

Here, we first start to create a **docker-compose.yaml** file:

```
version: '3.8'
services:
  wasm-app:
    build: .
    command: ["node", "scripts/wasm-server.js"]
    ports:
      - "8080:8080"
  wasm-app-dapr:
    image: "daprio/daprd:latest"
    depends_on:
      - wasm-app
    command: [
```

```
      "./daprd",
      "-app-id", "wasm-app",
      "-app-port", "8080",
      "-components-path", "/components"
    ]
    network_mode: "service:wasm-app"
    volumes:
      - ./config:/components
```

Then, we simply run:

```
docker-compose up
```

After this, both the Wasm app and Dapr sidecar run together, networking is handled for us, and the component files (state stores, pub/sub) are mounted into the sidecar.

Deploying on Kubernetes

For production, the Dapr shines when run as part of a Kubernetes cluster. In this model, the services (including Wasm hosts) are deployed as pods, and Dapr is injected as a sidecar container within the same pod.

Prepare Container Image

First, we start with the package of the Wasm host app as a Docker image:

```
docker build -t theuser/wasm-app:latest .
docker push theuser/wasm-app:latest
```

Write Kubernetes Deployment Manifest

Following is a simplified deployment YAML:

```
apiVersion: apps/v1
kind: Deployment
metadata:
  name: wasm-app
spec:
```

```yaml
  replicas: 2
  selector:
    matchLabels:
      app: wasm-app
  template:
    metadata:
      labels:
        app: wasm-app
      annotations:
        dapr.io/enabled: "true"
        dapr.io/app-id: "wasm-app"
        dapr.io/app-port: "8080"
    spec:
      containers:
      - name: wasm-app
        image: theuser/wasm-app:latest
        ports:
        - containerPort: 8080
```

The Dapr will automatically inject a sidecar and expose all APIs. And then, we apply the manifest using:

```
kubectl apply -f deployment.yaml
```

If you follow this simple process of getting the Wasm host into a container, adding the sidecar, and then deploying to Kubernetes or with Docker Compose, we can take Wasm and Dapr from local prototypes to cloud-scale reliability. Basically, this foundation lets us plug the business logic into any distributed system architecture supported by Dapr, making continuous delivery, monitoring, and scaling routine and predictable.

Summary

Overall, we learned to integrate WebAssembly modules into real-world cloud-native applications using Dapr. We learned to set up the Dapr environment both locally and for production, and packaged the Wasm code for Go and Python. We explored the practical workflows for building, exposing, and calling Wasm modules through Dapr service invocation API. The chapter then showed how Wasm can be used for decision engines and demonstrated bi-directional communication.

We learned the approaches for deploying Wasm-powered services with Docker Compose and Kubernetes, and then scaling them out and managing upgrades without deep infrastructure rewrites. This chapter successfully prepared us to move Wasm projects from standalone experiments into scalable, maintainable, and language-agnostic service architectures.

Chapter 9: Running WebAssembly Apps on Kubernetes

After learning how to harness Dapr for integrating WebAssembly into distributed, cloud-friendly architectures, our final step is to focus on the deployment and operation of WebAssembly applications at scale. We all know that the Kubernetes has emerged as the leading platform for automating deployment, scaling, and management of containerized applications.

In this chapter, we will practically skillup ourseleves to package, deploy, and manage WebAssembly workloads on Kubernetes. We will see the containerization techniques and learn to apply to Wasm hosts. We will learn to apply Kubernetes to carry out the networking, discovery, and scaling for the Wasm-powered microservices. We will learn about key operators and tools that simplify running Wasm workloads and expose powerful capabilities like auto-scaling, secrets management, and declarative configuration.

Packaging Wasm Apps for Kubernetes

The first thing to understand is the foundation, which is that to run WebAssembly workloads on Kubernetes, we first need to wrap the Wasm module in a host application that can launch and execute it. The thing is, Wasm itself is platform-neutral and doesn't run on its own, so it needs a runtime (like Wasmtime, Wasmer, or WasmEdge). Basically, we'll package this runtime as the ENTRYPOINT of the container, along with the Wasm binary.

So let us say that we have a Wasm module built from C, Rust, or AssemblyScript. We can place the **.wasm** file and the chosen runtime (for example, Wasmtime) inside a container image. We then can create a **Dockerfile** like this:

```
FROM debian:bullseye-slim

RUN apt-get update && apt-get install -y wget ca-certificates
&& \

    wget -O /usr/local/bin/wasmtime
https://github.com/bytecodealliance/wasmtime/releases/download
/v14.0.4/wasmtime-v14.0.4-x86_64-linux.tar.xz && \

    chmod +x /usr/local/bin/wasmtime

COPY dist/module.wasm /module.wasm

ENTRYPOINT ["/usr/local/bin/wasmtime", "/module.wasm"]
```

We then build and push this image to the container registry:

```
docker build -t theuser/wasm-module:latest .

docker push theuser/wasm-module:latest
```

After this, the image can now be referenced in the Kubernetes manifests. The key step is that the Wasm runtime becomes the container's main process, and the module is executed as soon as the pod starts. If the logic needs to expose networking (HTTP, gRPC), include scripts or small servers to handle requests and forward them to Wasm exports.

In the next topic, we will see how to actually deploy, expose, and manage these containers within a Kubernetes cluster.

Deploying Wasm Containers to Kubernetes

Once the Wasm module and runtime are packaged as a container image, we are ready to launch it on Kubernetes. The process is very similar to deploying any application as shown in the following steps.

Creating Kubernetes Deployment Manifest

We first create a deployment YAML file, such as **`wasm-module-deployment.yaml`**. This manifest describes how many replicas we want, how the pod should be labeled, and which container image to use:

```
apiVersion: apps/v1
kind: Deployment
metadata:
  name: wasm-module
spec:
  replicas: 2
  selector:
    matchLabels:
      app: wasm-module
  template:
    metadata:
      labels:
        app: wasm-module
    spec:
      containers:
```

```yaml
      - name: wasm-runtime
        image: theuser/wasm-module:latest
        ports:
        - containerPort: 8080 # If the runtime exposes HTTP
```

After this, we then apply this manifest to the cluster with:

```
kubectl apply -f wasm-module-deployment.yaml
```

The Kubernetes will pull the container, start the Wasm runtime, and execute the module in as many pods as you've specified (here, 2). We can verify pod status and see logs using:

```
kubectl get pods
kubectl logs <pod-name>
```

Exposing Wasm Service

If the Wasm host serves requests (HTTP/gRPC), we then create a Service object so other pods or external clients can access it. See the following example:

```yaml
apiVersion: v1
kind: Service
metadata:
  name: wasm-service
spec:
  selector:
    app: wasm-module
  ports:
  - protocol: TCP
    port: 80
    targetPort: 8080
  type: ClusterIP
```

We then apply the service:

```
kubectl apply -f wasm-service.yaml
```

After this, it gives us a stable network address like **wasm-service.default.svc.cluster.local** for the Wasm pods within the Kubernetes cluster.

Scaling and Rolling Updates

The Kubernetes makes it easy to scale the Wasm workloads. To increase replicas, we just need to update the deployment YAML or run:

```
kubectl scale deployment wasm-module --replicas=5
```

For updates, we can build new images and change the Deployment spec's image tag; then apply the update. The Kubernetes will safely roll out new pods and terminate old ones.

Managing Configuration and Secrets

Once the WebAssembly containers are running in Kubernetes, we will often need to supply them with configuration files, environment variables, or sensitive secrets like API keys. The Kubernetes provides built-in mechanisms for handling both general configuration and secrets securely and effectively without hardcoding anything in the image.

Using ConfigMaps

If the Wasm module or its host runtime needs certain settings, like a path to a file, feature flags, or endpoint URLs, we can store these values in a Kubernetes ConfigMap.

So, we create a simple ConfigMap YAML like this:

```
apiVersion: v1
kind: ConfigMap
metadata:
  name: wasm-config
  namespace: default
  labels:
    app: wasm-module

data:
```

```
  WASM_FEATURE_FLAG: "true"
  ENDPOINT_URL: "https://api.example.com"
```

We then apply it to the cluster:

```
kubectl apply -f wasm-config.yaml
```

Now here, to make these variables available to the container, we mount them as environment variables in the pod spec:

```
spec:
  containers:
  - name: wasm-runtime
    image: theuser/wasm-module:latest
    env:
    - name: WASM_FEATURE_FLAG
      valueFrom:
        configMapKeyRef:
          name: wasm-config
          key: WASM_FEATURE_FLAG
    - name: ENDPOINT_URL
      valueFrom:
        configMapKeyRef:
          name: wasm-config
          key: ENDPOINT_URL
```

After this, the Wasm app can read these values at startup and adjust its logic accordingly.

Supplying Secrets

For sensitive values (like passwords, tokens, or private keys), we can use Kubernetes Secrets. They look similar to ConfigMaps but encrypt data at rest within the cluster.

To do this, we create a secret like this:

```
apiVersion: v1
```

```
kind: Secret
metadata:
  name: wasm-secrets
  namespace: default
data:
  API_KEY: c2VjcmV0X3ZhbHVlCg==  # base64 encoded
"secret_value"
```

Then ,we apply:

```
kubectl apply -f wasm-secrets.yaml
```

After this, we then reference it in the container spec with the same **env** block method:

```
env:
  - name: API_KEY
    valueFrom:
      secretKeyRef:
        name: wasm-secrets
        key: API_KEY
```

To conclude, the host app reads configuration and secrets from the container's environment at startup and passes them or uses them as needed, when interacting with Wasm functions. This keeps sensitive data outside the source code and build process while making dynamic configuration management easy.

Handling Networking and Communication for Wasm Applications

Once the Wasm containers are running in Kubernetes and are configured with all needed settings and secrets, the next step is to ensure the modules can communicate with clients, other services, and external systems. The Kubernetes gives us flexible networking primitives so that the Wasm services can be discovered, accessed, and participate in distributed workflows.

Here, we will learn to make the WebAssembly-powered app available to the rest of the system and to the outside world. To do this, we just have to follow as shown below, and that too in the same order of steps:

Expose Wasm Pod inside Cluster

After we create a Deployment for the Wasm service (as we did in the previous topics), we expose it with a Kubernetes Service. For example, let us say that the Wasm-based HTTP server listens on port 8080. So here, we simply write a service manifest:

```
apiVersion: v1
kind: Service
metadata:
  name: wasm-service
spec:
  selector:
    app: wasm-module
  ports:
    - protocol: TCP
      port: 80
      targetPort: 8080
  type: ClusterIP
```

We then apply it with:

```
kubectl apply -f wasm-service.yaml
```

After this, any other service or pod running in the cluster can reach the Wasm application at this DNS address:

```
wasm-service.default.svc.cluster.local:80
```

So, even if we have a Go or Python service that needs to call the Wasm business logic, we need to just point the API client to that service DNS name and port 80, and the Kubernetes will automatically direct the request to the appropriate running pod.

Wasm App Accessibility

If the Wasm service should be reached from outside the cluster (for example: by mobile apps, web frontends, or external APIs), we then here need to expose it using a LoadBalancer or Ingress.

Let us take a quickest example as below:

In the following service YAML, we first set the type:

```
spec:
  type: LoadBalancer
```

The Kubernetes will assign a public IP address. Once the service is running, we get the address via:

```
kubectl get services
```

The **EXTERNAL-IP** column will show the service's public endpoint. We can now run:

```
curl http://<external-ip>/my-endpoint
```

to test the WebAssembly business logic from outside.

If we want more control over URLs or run on a private cluster, we can set up an Ingress resource. After installing an ingress controller, we can easily define a rule:

```
apiVersion: networking.k8s.io/v1
kind: Ingress
metadata:
  name: wasm-ingress
spec:
  rules:
    - host: wasmapp.mycompany.com
      http:
        paths:
          - path: /
            pathType: Prefix
            backend:
              service:
                name: wasm-service
                port:
                  number: 80
```

Now here, any request to **http://wasmapp.mycompany.com/** routes automatically to the Wasm-powered app.

Testing Connections

Here, we deploy all manifests. And then, to test internal access:

```
kubectl run -it --rm --restart=Never busybox --image=busybox
sh
# Inside the pod shell:
wget -qO- http://wasm-service:80/the-endpoint
```

Similarly, to test external connections, we then use the cURL against the external IP or Ingress host as shown below:

```
curl http://wasmapp.mycompany.com/the-endpoint
```

If something isn't reachable, we need to check the following:

- Are the service, deployment, and pods all healthy? (**kubectl get all**)
- Does the Wasm host process log any bind or permission errors?
- Are firewall rules or security groups blocking the service (cloud provider issues)?
- Does the Ingress controller have the correct hostname and TLS settings (for HTTPS)?

Basically, we just expose the Wasm workload to the cluster with a Service. We expose it to the outside world with LoadBalancer or Ingress. We test everything using the actual URLs and ports Kubernetes gives you. This setup makes the WebAssembly app really accessible, connectable and production-ready in Kubernetes.

Monitoring and Debugging Wasm Workloads

Once the Wasm application is live on Kubernetes and accessible through the network, the next practical challenge is keeping track of its health, diagnosing issues, and ensuring it runs reliably. The Kubernetes provides several tools and workflows for monitoring and debugging that we can use directly with the WebAssembly workloads.

Inspect Pod and Container Logs

We must understand that every Wasm workload is running inside a Kubernetes pod. So, to check what the application is doing or see errors reported by the Wasm host, we can use:

```
kubectl logs <pod-name>
```

If the deployment creates multiple pods, we can get their names with:

```
kubectl get pods
```

Now here, we must look for print statements, error logs, or custom debug output from the application or the runtime.

Check Pod Health and Status

The Kubernetes manages the lifecycle of the pods. We can check if everything is running as expected:

```
kubectl get pods
```

After this, the Pods stuck in **`CrashLoopBackOff`** or **`Error`** might indicate bugs in the Wasm app, wrong command arguments, or misconfigured startup settings.

Use of Liveness and Readiness Probes

To help Kubernetes automatically restart failed Wasm apps, we simply add the liveness and readiness probes to the deployment. For example, if the Wasm HTTP server listens on **`/healthz`**, we then include:

```
livenessProbe:
  httpGet:
    path: /healthz
    port: 8080
  initialDelaySeconds: 5
  periodSeconds: 10
readinessProbe:
  httpGet:
    path: /healthz
    port: 8080
  initialDelaySeconds: 2
  periodSeconds: 3
```

With this, the Kubernetes will automatically remove and restart unhealthy pods, ensuring the service stays available.

Kubernetes Dashboard Monitoring

For a graphical overview, we can simply enable the Kubernetes Dashboard. It displays pod health, resource usage, and error messages. To do this, we simply install and access it with the following script:

```
kubectl apply -f
https://raw.githubusercontent.com/kubernetes/dashboard/v2.7.0/
aio/deploy/recommended.yaml

kubectl proxy
```

We can also visit **http://localhost:8001/api/v1/namespaces/kubernetes-dashboard/services/https:kubernetes-dashboard:/proxy/** in the browser to do the same.

If issues can't be resolved by logs or dashboard info, we can check the following tricks:

- Review environment variables for missing config or secrets
- Verify all dependencies are present inside the pod (correct image build)
- Confirm networking setup matches service and port definitions
- Restart pods for a clean state:

```
kubectl rollout restart deployment/wasm-module
```

This hands-on workflow helps us catch problems early, gets the Wasm service back online quickly, and gives us confidence in running production-grade workloads.

Summary

To sum up, we learned to run the WebAssembly applications as scalable services inside Kubernetes clusters. We packaged the Wasm module with a host runtime into a standard container image and pushed it to a registry for deployment. We created the Kubernetes Deployment manifests to launch multiple replicas and used Services to expose the Wasm application for both internal communication and external access by clients. We managed the configuration and secrets securely using ConfigMaps and Secrets.

Later, we learned to connect the Wasm-based pods to other services and expose endpoints using load balancers or ingress rules for real-world accessibility. We managed to monitor and troubleshoot the Wasm workloads by inspecting logs, checking pod health, and using probes and the Kubernetes dashboard. Throughout the chapter, we built a clear workflow for integrating Wasm modules into large systems, making cloud-native Wasm applications easier to operate and maintain.

Index

Epilogue

It looks like you've made it. It's a big step from learning the basics of WebAssembly to getting workloads ready for production on Kubernetes. What you have now are skills that most developers are only just starting to explore, so you are ahead of the game. What I want you to remember is that, the WebAssembly isn't just another passing technology trend. It's already being used by Adobe, Figma, Google and many other companies to solve real problems. These chapters cover learning memory management, building multi-threaded apps, migrating legacy code, integrating with Dapr, and orchestrating on Kubernetes. These are all practical, real-world exercises. These are the exact skills teams are looking for right now.

So what happens next? You should build something. You should use WebAssembly to make that side project you've been thinking about. For example, if you migrate a slow JavaScript module, you can see the difference when it runs ten times faster. You can experiment with edge computing, game engines, blockchain nodes, or scientific simulations. The ecosystem is growing fast, and there's room for your ideas. And keep on learning, building and connecting with the WebAssembly community. You can follow the W3C working groups, contribute to open-source runtimes and share your experiments. This technology will keep on improving, with new ideas, better equipment and more ways to use it. I'm really looking forward to seeing what you construct. If this book helped you solve a problem or achieve something meaningful, then that's exactly why I wrote it. I'm grateful you chose me to support you on your learning journey.

Have fun and make something amazing!

- Emrys Callahan

Thank You

www.ingramcontent.com/pod-product-compliance
Lightning Source LLC
Chambersburg PA
CBHW080216170726
48282CB00030B/1138